*Moses
in
the
Twentieth
Century*

*

A
UNIVERSAL
PRIMER

Moses
in the
Twentieth Century

A UNIVERSAL PRIMER

Susan Roth

SJR ASSOCIATES
Springfield, New Jersey

$^7/_{94}$

Design and production by Arvid Knudsen & Associates
Cover design by DAK Graphics
Cover illustration by Art Seiden
Electronic type by Desktop Emporium
Printed and bound in the United States by Horowitz/Rae Book
    Manufacturers, Inc.

#24.95

TXU592433 1994
ISBN 0-9638861-0-X TX

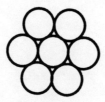

This book is dedicated
to the life of
Anne Frank

TIME BY ITSELF HAS NO MEANING AND NO PURPOSE

For the human race, time is a journey we take in space. It is we, the human race, who give time meaning and purpose by the way we use it. If we use it for creative and constructive purposes, purposes that better us as a species and improve the world we live in, then we have used time wisely. Then we can take our place among the stars of the universe. If, however, we use it for selfish and frivolous purposes, to glorify only one part of mankind at the expense of the rest, then we have wasted time foolishly. Then time has lost its purpose, and we have lost ourselves!

Contents

ACKNOWLEDGEMENTS

Before I give credit or thanks to anyone, I must thank God, the Almighty, for having given us the fax.

As I was faxing this manuscript to my editor, from Jerusalem to New York, I knew that without the fax machine I would not have been able to complete this undertaking.

But the more I wrote, and the more I faxed, the more I realized that the fax is not something man invented at all. Rather, the good Lord created everything that exists in this universe at the beginning of time (*Bereishit*). Our role, through science, was and is to discover how to put everything together to make this world a better place. Then we, like God, can stand back, look and say, "It is good; it works."

It eventually occurred to me that the first fax ever sent came from God to Moses on Mount Sinai. That fax was the Ten Commandments, transmitted with pure energy (our fax machines use energy as well).

It took us mortals so long to harness energy in this way because the wisdom and knowledge required to do so eluded us when Moses, seeing the Israelites behaving in a wild and immature fashion, was compelled to break the first set of tablets as he descended Mount Sinai. His people were not ready for the kind of energy sent for them to receive. In Hebrew, the word *Kabbalah* means reception, from the word *lekabel* (to receive). And so,

Moses had to go back up Mount Sinai to bring the Torah down to the Children of Israel, this time in long hand.

Thank God, we finally have evolved and matured enough to understand what we were supposed to grasp in the first place. And perhaps that is why this generation is so hungry for the knowledge of *Kabbalah*.[1]

Perhaps we are finally ready to receive the Tree of Life and create a Garden of Eden here on earth for our generation and for those to come.

* * *

Now it is time to thank the many mortals who deserve my gratitude and love for helping me reach this point. Over the past nineteen years, they were my support system. Unfortunately, with so many people to thank, it would be impossible for me to name them all. But you all know who you are and that there is a part of each and every one of you in this book.

One person, however, whom I must thank by name is Rabbi Moshe Ben-Yehudah. His brilliant scholarship substantiated my claims through primary sources, some of which are not known even to many rabbis and great scholars. I also wish to thank him for his extraordinarily illuminating epilogue.

I must especially thank my copy editor, Chava Levy, for sifting diligently through nineteen years of cobwebs to reveal the diamond I started out with in 1975. Last, but not least, I am grateful to Arvid Knudsen, who helped me to polish it up for publication.

My deepest gratitude goes to my family for bearing with me through thick and thin these past nineteen years. I could not have written this book without their support and understanding.

Susan Roth
Erev Shabbat Kodesh, 15 Sivan, 5754
May 15, 1994

PREFACE

I f Moses could be with us today in the twentieth century, I feel
sure that he would say to us: "Children, it grieves me to see
that you did not understand the message I gave you 3,500 years
ago at Mount Sinai, a message that was, in fact, a blueprint of the
Unified Universe in which you live as Adam, male/female[2], in a
balanced, binary state.[3]

"The first set of tablets I received for you was so simple, and
yet it contained all the Wisdom that exists. Those tablets were
to have guided you in your journey through time and space.

"Obviously, your species was not mature enough to integrate
so much Wisdom, Wisdom that is the essence of *Kabbalah*.
Instead, I had to impart that same Wisdom to you in a container
of five books, layered like an onion, to be peeled by you, layer by
layer, until hopefully you would see the light.[4]

"The key, however, was, is and always will be the same:
Wisdom. And the part of Adam that was programmed with that
Wisdom from the beginning was — and is — the female aspect
of Adam: Woman - *Isha*.

"How unfortunate that in her quest for equality, she tried to
become just like the male aspect of Adam: Man - *Ish*. In doing
so, she forgot her vital role as 'Keeper of the Flame.'[5]

"As your century draws to a close, it is imperative that all
women use the gift they received at birth, the key of Wisdom, to
open the doors of the twenty-first century for all mankind.

"The *Eshet Chayil* (Woman of Valor) of the twenty-first century must balance the scale of Torah for the Jewish and non-Jewish world alike. She must expose the true meaning and purpose of Torah in an ever-expanding global society.

"The *Eshet Chayil* of today is the twenty-first century Eve: the feminine aspect of Adam. It is she who will determine what kind of world awaits us. Her choices of Good over Evil will steer humanity from a path of destruction to one of rebirth.

"Twenty-first century Eve at last must eat the fruit of the Tree of Life, that is, Torah. In doing so, she will awaken within herself and all of Humanity the Wisdom of Torah, ensuring the continuation of life on this fragile planet that we call Home."

The foundation of all foundations (and basic
principles of Torah) and the pillar of all
wisdoms is to know that there is a First Being
Who brings every existing thing into being.
All existing things — in heaven, on earth, and
what is between them — come into being only
from His true existence.
If it should enter one's mind that He does not exist —
no other thing could have any existence.
Mishneh Torah, Yesodei HaTorah, 1:1-2

Blessed is the man who finds Wisdom,
the man who gains understanding,
for she is more profitable than silver
and yields better returns than gold.
She is more precious than rubies;
nothing you desire can compare with her.
Long life is in her right hand;
in her left hand are riches and honor.
Her ways are pleasant ways, and all her paths are Peace.
She is a Tree of Life to those who embrace her,
those who lay hold of her will be blessed.
Proverbs 3:13-18

By wisdom the Lord laid the earth's foundations.

Proverbs 3:19A

Woman of Valor, who can find?
For she is more precious than rubies and pearls.
She opens her mouth with Wisdom,
and the teaching of kindness is on her tongue.

Proverbs 31:10,26

AUTHOR'S FOREWORD

Nineteen years ago, I acknowledged — and accepted — the very distinct possibility of a nuclear holocaust. It seemed to me that mankind, in its search for that elusive "Tree of Life," had learned not only to create life in the laboratory, but to destroy all life forms outside the laboratory. Our inhabitants, and our planet itself, were at risk.

Our planet, in fact, was not alone. Also in imminent danger was the entire universe, a space that functions as its name would suggest: universe, a verse that is uni. By this I mean a unified group, or verse, of planets that function as a unified whole, in synchronicity. In other words, the universe represents a oneness of many facets that are in perfect balance.

Frustrated by my inability to alter our world's political and military hostilities, fearful that I had no say in events that could destroy my family and its offspring, I felt compelled to do something. I remembered our astronauts returning from outer space. One by one, they described the view from on high as one of "majesty," "beauty," "awe." They felt a oneness with this planet, a planet that they referred to as "Spaceship Earth," a "global village" that they saw floating in Space and Time.

Unlike the astronauts, those of us who had never left the earth's stratosphere were unconscious of this oneness. To experience it, we had to turn to the teachings of the highest schools of learning.

We humans certainly had become scientific, sophisticated and highly specialized in technology, yet starving, drought-ridden, and homeless on the other. This dichotomy was also reflected in paradoxical statements within various academic disciplines.

Sociologists, anthropologists, economists and natural scientists were not engaging in serious dialogue about the problems facing our planet, as a whole. International and academic politics began to merge, resulting in a serious turning point for myself and many other concerned writers of the late 1970's and early 1980's.

Fritjof Capra was one of those concerned writers exploring this new phenomenon. In the introduction to his book, *The Turning Point: Science, Society, and the Rising Culture* (1982), he quoted from the *I Ching*:

> After a time of decay comes the turning point. The powerful light which has been banished returns. There is movement, but it is not brought about by force ... The movement is natural, arising spontaneously. For the transformation becomes easy. The old is discarded and the new introduced. Both measures accord with the time; therefore no harm results.[6]

Ken Wilbur echoed these sentiments in *Up From Eden* (1981). He claimed we had entered a "New Age" that necessitated a more unified view of humanity, one that would enable it to keep growing as a cohesive species, in tune with its environment. Fortunately, Mr. Wilbur was not the only one reminding us that we were destroying the only home we have. Gregory Bateson and others contributed to our awareness, showing how important it was for ecologists and anthropologists to confer with each other and with architects, economists and politicians, creating better and safer societies in the process.

I was convinced that the academic community had to reevaluate its *raison d'etre*. Processing information for its own sake, especially when that information was emerging at such a rapid rate, was absurd. Academia had to adopt a dual approach to the knowledge it was assimilating. While continuing to promote specialization, it could not risk ignoring the forest for the trees. The academic community had to process and assess and apply the proliferating information about ourselves and our universe. The human race depended on it.

As I saw it, the past, present and future were all one, as are we, and what humanity had always attempted was to strike a proper balance through Time in Space for the survival of the species. Furthermore, I became convinced that we humans had developed a sixth sense — one of doom. That sense had to be eradicated, lest it destroy the human race through a prophetic wish.

At that moment, I resolved to make a contribution — no matter how slight - towards our survival, not just for my family, but for all humankind. Not surprisingly, as a professional educator, I chose academics as the bailiwick for that contribution.

My involvement with eastern and western mystical traditions had helped me to detect the unifying threads of the universe. I had to convey this sense of unity to others, particularly within the academic community.

I am sure that many academicians, convinced that their specialty is the panacea for all our ills, will feel threatened by my assertion that only an interdisciplinary approach will solve our problem. After all, isn't that what academics has always been about? As Fritjof Capra reminds us in *The Tao of Physics* (1975), "The roots of all Western science are to be found in the first period of Greek philosophy in the sixth century B.C., in a culture where science, philosophy and religion were not separated." The sages were not concerned with the distinction, but rather with the essential nature, of things.

Perhaps we have come to a point where we do understand the nature of all things but have forgotten their interconnectedness. If this is so, then perhaps we have reached an era when we can begin to unify these two views into a whole picture of ourselves. Perhaps we can begin to see ourselves as we really are and not simply as we would like to think we are.

ANNOTATOR'S FOREWORD

I take pride in introducing the book Moses in the Twentieth Century. It is a unique work, written in straightforward language that can be understood by everyone. Its message is simple and to the point: It's high time all of us woke up and noticed what's happening in our world. Its message is profound: Even though we all differ from one another, each with our own personal identity and each subscribing to our own particular Wisdom, there is nevertheless an underlying unity connecting all of us as a greater whole. This unity runs through the entire universe.

Amazingly, although interconnected at this deeper level, we never lose our unique individuality. This phenomenon is what I call "Unified Dualism."

Deeply inspired by Torah sources, author Susan Roth wrote this book without access to ancient Kabbalistic texts or the Talmud and Mishnah in their original Hebrew and Aramaic forms. She sent me the manuscript for proofreading and annotation of Torah sources. Seriously involved in Jewish mysticism, I realized over the years that *Kabbalah* — the core of the Torah - is also an all-encompassing meta-system for understanding the world's different wisdoms. Our Rabbis alluded to this notion in the Mishnah:

Turn it and turn it again, for everything is in it (*Avot* 5:22).

In other words, only after constant diligence, only after delving into the depths of Torah as a whole, will one merit understanding how this is so.

Annotating this work was a rare, exciting opportunity. When the author combined Torah and secular sources to substantiate her thesis, and when she took a stand on controversial issues, the wisdom of Torah was brought to the fore in all its splendor.

Many Orthodox Jews might find the ideas presented here strange, even foreign to Torah tradition. That is simply because these concepts come from the esoteric part of Torah, with which many are not familiar. Nevertheless, the reader will see that the author's presentation is very logical and certainly holds water. For optimal comprehension, the book should be studied in conjunction with its epilogue and footnotes. It is important to read carefully through the entire book.

I am especially pleased to have collaborated on *Moses in the Twentieth Century* because it shows how Torah and science - two entirely different disciplines - interconnect and, at their deepest level, can become one. I am also pleased to show, albeit briefly, that the axioms of quantum physics are subsumed in *Kabbalah*.

This volume illustrates that we are living in very unique times. It is our hope that this modest work will serve as a stepping stone, enabling each reader to achieve greater spiritual growth.

Rabbi Moshe Ben-Yehudah

PART I

Moses in the
Twentieth Century

Rendevous with Destiny

Yes, there is such a thing as destiny. No, it is not what most people imagine, such as winning a lottery or meeting their knight in shining armor.

Destiny is the process that brings you face to face with your life's purpose. Making numerous decisions, including choices of good over evil, are only steps bringing you to your rendezvous with destiny.

Since my rendezvous began in 1975, when I composed *Moses in the Twentieth Century*, it seemed only natural that I should begin Part One with this very special poem to complete one chapter of fate and to lead into the next one.

The Question

I was not taught to be with THEE
I only knew I wished to be,
and then one day YOU came to me
and said, "I AM ALL THAT YOU SEE
UN* AM I." YOU also said,
"COME WALK WITH ME AND BE A PART OF ALL
    YOU SEE."

* UN, pronounced YUN, means The Unified One.

II

UN took me here and took me there
I know that I knew everywhere,
and when that day was finally done
I knew that UNE and we were ONE.

III

I walked with UN from dusk till dawn
until the Moon became the Sun,
twas almost like before "The Fall,"
again I saw that UNE was ALL.

IV

I can't believe what I have seen
a miracle, or so it seems,
to see the world as just a walk,
could it have started as a spark?

V

UN said we started as a thought,
as everything Man ever sought,
and so I too began to think.
Another World was on the brink.

VI

Yes WISDOM was what I had learned
when I was finally returned,
but if I try to spread the word
I'll have a hard time, so I've heard.

VII

Now I must say "UN, please brief me
when asked from whence comes my degree,
how can I say it came from thee,
WISDOM it's called, and ALL YOU SEE?"

VIII

They'll laugh at me and say in short,
"that's not enough for Man today for doubters we have all become,
how can we know there's only UN?
There are those worshipping the 'SON' and others knowing more
*   than One."*

IX

"Our universities are here
to teach you LIFE from everywhere,
you can't get your degree from UNE
there's always new under the Sun."

X

And so I ask of you dear UN
what say I to those with degrees from famous universities,
who know their Theses oh so well
but as for WISDOM fail to tell?

The Answer

I

"YOU'LL BE A STUDENT THEY CAN SEE
AND IN A UNIVERSITY
WITH TEXTBOOK NOTES ON HUMAN NEED
IT'S TIME TO TEACH ABOUT THE SEED

II

OF TRUTH YOU'LL WRITE
AND USE A NAME THAT'S MORTAL
YES YOU'LL PLAY THE GAME
THAT'S PLAYED AGAIN TIME IN TIME OUT
THROUGH CENTURIES OF TIMELESS DROUGHT

III

AND WHEN THE WORLD CANNOT GET WORSE
UNE COMES TO ONE AND SAYS REHEARSE
THE LINES WITH WHICH TO WRITE THE PLAY
FOR MAN TO UNDERSTAND THE WAY

IV

IN PAST 'TWAS EASIER THAN NOW
THE WORLD CAN'T CEASE TO GROW AND GROW
IN LEAPS AND BOUNDS IT JOINS THE NILE
WHILE GETTING SMALLER ALL THE WHILE

V

I AM UN, PLEASE GET A PEN
YOU MUST RETELL THE PLAY AGAIN
BUT NOW THE PAGES ARE NOT TEN
THEY'RE ALTOGETHER ONCE AGAIN

VI

THE JIGSAW PUZZLE THEY WILL SEE
WHEN YOU PRESENT THEM WITH MY KEY
WHILE USING LANGUAGE THEY CAN SEE
FROM THEIR OWN UNIVERSITY."

VII

To tell the truth, I must confess.
I feel not only mere distress
I don't know if I'm better off
than those who knew UNE in TIME's droughts,

VIII

and can't help turning all my thoughts
to all those years when Life was shy,
it had not blossomed yet our way
when people wanted to expand their minds into your Foreign Land.

IX

"PAST MESSENGERS EACH HAD ONE TASK
TO TEACH THEIR PEOPLE HOW TO ASK
THE QUESTIONS THAT WOULD LEAD THE WAY
FOR ALL THE PATHWAYS OF TODAY

X

NOW YOU'RE THE ONE TO WHOM I SAY
GO SHOW THEM THERE'S ANOTHER WAY
WHERE ALL ROADS MEET AND IN A WHILE
THEY'LL REUNITE ALONG THE NILE."

XI

I'll walk with UN through night and day
while learning in another way
to show the world that we're all ONE
all different pieces of a sum.

XII

I'll say, that it's not only us
but all that is and ever was,
PAST, PRESENT, FUTURE, all are one,
TIME is a circle to be done.

XIII

And numbers that are infinite,
are only so within the light
that's given to us by the Sun,
of course it's also part of UN.

XIV

Now is the time to fill Man's cup
so we don't blow each other up,
I hope we learn our lesson well
so we may live the time to tell:

XV

A play was given us to read
and with it came a GOLDEN SEED,
it grew as we spoke out the lines
as actors in a play that rhymes.

XVI

The SEED took hold in everyone,
and grew to bind us as a tree.
"A TREE OF LIFE we've all become,
and know deep down that ALL is UN."

Time

The preservation of the Jew was certainly not casual. He has endured through the power of a certain ideal, based upon the recognition of the influence of a Higher Power in human affairs. Time after time in his history, moreover, he has been saved from disaster in a manner which cannot be described excepting as 'providential.' The author has deliberately attempted to write this work in a secular spirit; he does not think that his readers can fail to see in it, on every page, a higher immanence.

Cecil Roth, A History of the Jews (p. 424)

The historian should take into account all forms of evidence, including those which are or appear to be metaphysical. If the earliest Jews were able to survey, with us, the history of their progeny, they would find nothing surprising in it. They always knew that Jewish society was appointed to be a pilot-project for the entire human race. That Jewish dilemmas, dreams and catastrophes should be exemplary, larger than life, would seem only natural to them. That Jews should over the millennia attract such unparalleled, indeed inexplicable, hatred would be regrettable but only to be expected. Above all, that the Jews should still survive, when all those other ancient peoples were transmuted or vanished into the oubliettes of history, was wholly predictable. How could it be otherwise? Providence decreed it and the Jews obeyed.

Paul Johnson, History of the Jews (pp. 586-587)

Time and the Calendar in Ancient Egypt

*I*t was here at Karnak that He who is called Amon sat upon
a hillock and thought the world into being during the
floods of the month of July. Here was conceived, and lived,
the Great Week of the Creation of the World, and the
Separation of the Earth from the Waters. You are in the
House of the Father. This Land is said to have been the
first to have risen from the Primeval Waters.
I, Amon, am the Father of Fathers, the Mother of Mothers,
and the Bull of the Seven Celestial Kine. I opened my
Mouth to speak in the midst of silence.
I caused to be that men should have a path on which to tread.
I opened the eyes of all, that they might see.
My right eye is the Day.
My left eye is the Night.
And the waters of the Nile spurt from my sandals to give Life.

*Excerpts from Egyptian mythological story of Creation
compiled by Egyptian scholars
for Thebes of The Hundred Gates*

When one looks at this account of Creation, one has to acknowledge its similarity to the biblical story of Genesis. Of course, they were given at two different times, but could they have shared a common origin?

The more one studies ancient Egyptian and Jewish history, one must realize that they share a unique bond. Egypt flourished at about the same time that a *Habiru* nomad, with expertise in astronomy and the cycles of nature, helped save that nation from a great famine. This *Habiru*, subsequently made Grand Vizier by the Pharaoh, brought his entire family to Egypt to live in the land of Giza. Biblical, archeological and Egyptian scholars concur that this *Habiru* was probably Joseph of the Bible and that he and his family were ancestors of the Hebrew slaves who built Egypt's great monuments, most of which stand to this day.[7]

As one examines the facts more deeply, one notes that these slaves were not one group of nomads but a number of groups that became, in time, an integral part of the Egyptian people. They multiplied greatly and shared many myths and beliefs about a god that one day would save them. These Hebrews were comprised of twelve tribes, the descendants of Abraham, Isaac and Jacob. Jacob, also known as Israel, was Joseph's father. With his entire family, he had emigrated to Egypt at Joseph's bidding.

Virtually all historians point to a moment in Egyptian history when a very large group of people left Egypt all at once. The Bible speaks of this as the Exodus. The Bible also claims that it was an Egyptian prince, himself a Hebrew, who received a divine call to free these slaves and create a nation that would worship the true God, YHVH.

These events seem to have coincided with the start of Egypt's decline and with the establishment of a calendar by this new nation of what I call Egyptian Hebrews.

This information underscores how intertwined were the historical accounts of Time and the establishment of the calendar for the ancient Egyptians and the nation they enslaved.

The ancient Egyptians seem to have evolved from two distinct groups. The first were nomadic agricultural peasants, unaware of the Nile. They simply knew that the river gave them life-sustaining waters needed to plant their crops. These people were at the mercy of nature's forces - and their own ignorance.

The second group apparently arrived on the scene sometime after 3400 B.C.E. They had advanced skills in astronomy, astrology, mathematics, medicine, geometry and mysticism. They became the priests and Pharaohs of Upper and Lower Egypt. Archaeological evidence shows that these newcomers were bigger-boned and taller than the primitive natives. These new rulers also introduced a new practice of mummifying the dead.[8]

These priests also figured out when the Nile would rise, based on their astronomical discovery that the dog star, Sothis (or Sirius, as we have come to call it), would reappear in the eastern sky, just before sunrise, after many months of invisibility. They saw that a great flood would then occur, beginning a cycle of twelve moons with five overlapping days before the flooding. They called this cycle a year, with the beginning of the year known as the time of the beginning of Creation.

The priests divided this pattern of twelve moons and five days (before the reappearance of Sothis) into three seasons: *Aket*, the time of flooding; *Proyet*, the time of sowing; and *Shomy*, the time of harvest. These times were known as months and the extra five days were called the Holiday of *Opet*. This yearly cycle became a civil calendar, used mainly for agricultural and trade purposes. It was a lunar calendar based on the ebb and flow of the Nile, consisting of twelve 30-day months with five concluding days. This lunar calendar became the ruling force for the Egyptian peasants. They were its slaves, with no day of rest incorporated into it. Their existence as individuals had no meaning whatso-ever. Their value was calculated only by how much work they could do - and how quickly they could do it.

In contrast, the aristocratic priests and pharaohs marked their time with the sun, whose daily rising and setting gave meaning and structure to their entire empire. The sun's appearance and departure structured their belief in life and death and fed their obsession with becoming immortal gods and goddesses. For them, the moon was the force controlling animals and vegetation. It seemed logical to them that slaves, in their eyes of no greater value than animals, should also be governed by that force. They, however, self-proclaimed offspring of gods and goddesses, expected to be governed by the sun, that superior force that reappeared each day. They were convinced that the sun marked time between the netherworlds, denoting eternal Time and Space.

The Pharaohs, obsessed with immortality, used the priests' mystical teachings to build two cities, symbolic of life and death, called Luxor-Karnak and Thebes, built on opposite sides of the Nile. The city of the living was on the east bank (where the sun rose) and the city of the dead was on the west bank (where the sun set). In Luxor, huge temples and monuments were built, as each Pharaoh attempted to outdo his predecessor. In Thebes, they built two valleys, one for the kings and one for the queens, with royal tombs embedded in the mountains. Each tomb had many chambers with walls featuring sacred representations of the netherworld, to which the deceased king, as companion of the sun god Ra, would sail daily. The netherworld was divided into 12 hours of the night that corresponded to the other 12 hours of the day. These hours were calculated by the priests-astronomers using the north-south, east-west dimensions of the pyramids.[9]

No one but the Pharaohs and priests knew of these tombs, no one, that is, except those who constructed them. Once they completed their labors, these workers were killed to protect the aristocrats' secret.

In effect, the rulers of Egypt tried to stop time through the use of a time capsule that housed their eternal souls and mortal bodies. They also tried to build time capsules to externalize the land of Egypt. These took the form of pyramids, the Sphinx, *Abu Symbal* and all the other great Egyptian monuments. And indeed they withstood the test of time. Scholars continue to study each monument in an attempt to understand its concept of time.

In retrospect, we see that the ancient Egyptians' attempt at timekeeping, through their study of lunar and solar cycles, was one of Man's earliest attempts to create a working calendar. We have, however, no lasting remains of either calendar, since neither was ever recorded for posterity. All we have are empty tombs and empty pyramids.

In conclusion, the aristocrats of ancient Egypt believed that the only lives that had any worth were their own. For them, time was a brief span between life and death, with only the netherworld having any lasting meaning, a meaning that was granted supposedly to a select few. Unfortunately, this meaning has been found to be as empty as their tombs, unearthed by a future generation they had hoped to reach through the resurrection promised in their myths of time.[10]

> ... the great, the mighty God,
> the Lord of Hosts is His name.
> ... Which did set signs and wonders
> in the land of Egypt even unto
> this day.
>
> *Jeremiah 32:18-20*

Time and the Calendar for the Hebrew Culture

*T*o everything there is a season,
and a time to every purpose under
the Heavens. A time to be born
and a time to die.

Ecclesiastes 2:2-3

... the great, the mighty God,
the Lord of Hosts is His name.
... Which did set signs and wonders
in the land of Egypt, even unto this day.

Jeremiah 32:18-20

The sun to rule the day and the moon to rule the night.

Genesis 1:18

According to the Baal Shem Tov (Master of the Good Name), the great mystical sage and founder of the Hasidic movement, each of us should believe that we — and the entire world — are re-created each morning. Our faith thus increased, we will take a fresh interest in our daily service to the Lord.[11]

According to an another great sage, Rabbi Nachman of Breslov, "Declare at all times: 'The world was created for my sake.' Do not declare: 'Of what concern is this to me?' But do your share to add some improvement, to supply something missing, and to leave the world a little better for your sojourn in it."[12]

According to the Vilna Gaon, each letter in the first word of Genesis — Bereishit (meaning "to begin with") — hints at the ingredients needed to be a person of goodness: Bet stands for bitachon (trust); Resh for ratzon (will); Aleph for ahavah (love); Shin for shtikah (silence); Yud for yir'ah (fear); and Tav for Torah (learning).

The second word in Genesis, bara (meaning "created") reminds us of our three most precious possessions: (1) children, from the word bar (son); (2) health, from bari (healthy); (3) food, from bar (grain). Continuing in this word-by-word fashion, the phrase Bereishit bara Elohim (God created), suggests that the Creation can only rest on truth because the last letters of these three words spell emet (truth).[13]

These exemplary quotes, a mere handful of the thousands of commentaries on the Jew's relationship to Creation and time, underscore a fundamental Jewish principle: Existence is purposeful and, consequently, man/woman has a purpose in life.

(The term "man/woman" is used here because Adam, Genesis's word for man, means "of the earth" or what I call "an earthling." Adam signifies both male and female, not unlike the Taoist Mandala of Yin/Yang, signifying the opposing creative forces found together in a perfectly balanced unit.)

Furthermore, these quotes illustrate how the Jew regards life in relation to time, which began (according to Genesis) 5753 years ago with the creation of all things by God, the One Perfect and Absolute Unity, the Creator of Time and Space.[14] All things included time and space, as we know them, in their finite form. According to Torah, everything that we can comprehend with our finite mind is finite, but theTimelessTime and Spaceless Space that are part of God's light which always is. This infinitude can be comprehended only through the mystical experiences described in the Hebrew tradition known as *Kabbalah*.

According to the Torah, God created the Universe in six stages, called days. God rested on the seventh day, a day that was — and is — His day: Divine and Holy. Because God created Man/Woman in His own image (an image that was also Male/Female, perhaps the primary Binary System of the Universe), He decreed that this entity do the same: create during six days of the week and rest on the seventh. This seventh day was, for Man/Woman, outside of their ordinary space/time.

To enable us to keep track of time as we know it, God created a sun and moon to denote the separation of day and night. The day began at sunset and ended with the following sunset. The sun and moon distinguished between light and darkness; served as omens; defined days, weeks, months and years; and determined festivals. Just as the day began with darkness, so did the month, whose beginning was, and still is, heralded by the New Moon.

This account of creation, as well as the rest of the Torah, was dictated by God to a man named Moses. Who was this extraordinary man? He was a product of two worlds: born in Egypt to an impoverished family of Levites (and an enslaved Hebrew nation); raised in the lap of luxury as a prince in Pharaoh's palace. Discreetly, young Moses maintained contact with his family and thus (as recorded in the Bible and *Midrash*) was inculcated with his Hebrew tradition. Moses was privy to all the mystical teachings of the Egyptian priests; he knew their hypotheses about Nature, about the lunar and solar cycles, about Time Space. He was tutored in the disciplines of astronomy, astrology, geometry and medicine.

It was this product of poverty and privilege, of piety and paganism, who became the Jewish nation's greatest prophet and leader. A man of extreme modesty, Moses led 600,000 Hebrew men (aged 20-60) into the Sinai Desert where they wandered for forty years. With them were women, children below the age of twenty and men over the age of sixty, bringing the Hebrew population to approximately three million. Moses also led out of Egypt a group of at least three million Egyptian converts known as the "Mixed Multitude."[15] He did this, according to the Torah, because of God's mandate to free the Hebrew slaves and make them one people, one nation that would worship the Unified God, YHVH. At the foot of Mount Sinai, God revealed Himself to these people and gave them a Torah based on Ten Divine Emanations, or Ten Commandments, as we call them.

These millions, representing a mix of Egypt's population, were told in very specific terms how to observe Time from that day forward, as well as what the "Head of the Months" should be for them. They were told that from that moment on they were to consider the night before the Exodus as Passover Night, when God killed all first-born Egyptian males, but saved from such a fate the Hebrews, who had put God's sign of Life (blood) on their doorposts. They were to commemorate this Exodus every year, generation after generation, by retelling the story of their slavery and redemption.[16]

These newly formed Israelites were told by God, through Moses, that the Ten Commandments were representative of the Ten Emanations that comprised the *Tree of Life* in the Garden of Eden, and thus they were, in essence, the entire Torah of Creation. They were then given 613 *mitzvot*-commandments (the deeper meaning of *mitzvah* - singular form of *mitzvot* — is connection and union), of which the following were particularly relative to Time:

1) Refraining from work on the Sabbath, the seventh day of the week.[17]

2) Counting seven weeks of the *Omer* as a Wave Offering, beginning on the second night of Passover (Pesach), the first major holiday of the year,[18] and sacrificing a Meal Offering to God on the fifth day.

3) Holding a Holy Convocation to God on the first day of the seventh month (*Rosh Hashanah*) and atoning for all their sins ten days later (*Yom Kippur*).

4) Observing a week-long Festival of Booths (*Sukkot*) to remember how God sheltered them in the desert.[19]

5) Observing a Sabbatical every seventh year, and a Jubilee every fifth year, to remember that all slaves and all inherited properties are to be set free.[20]

Twelve Tribes were established, each named for one of Jacob's descendants, who had been in Egypt for 210 years. These twelve names are associated with the twelve lunar months, upon which the Hebrew calendar is based. The beginning of each month, associated with the empty, receptive moon, was to be blessed, while the full moon would give its energy during the major festivals.

The rising and setting of the sun became times for specific blessings. The twelve tribes also are associated with the twelve astrological signs linked to each lunar month.[21] The children of Israel were to observe this calendar not only to track the cycles of nature, but also to commemorate their history, going all the way back to Abraham and his Covenant with God, representing the first Time-bound *mitzvah* in a Jewish male's life: circumcision, to be performed at the age of eight days.

As they evolved, the Jewish people continued to imbue time with meaning. Approximately 2,000 years ago, Ezra the scribe instructed them to read one portion of the Torah on every Sabbath. To this day, in houses of worship the world over Jews celebrate *Simchat Torah* by hearing the conclusion of Deuteronomy, immediately followed by the first portion of Genesis. This seamless reading cycle reinforces their conviction that God's time has no beginning and no end. Genesis was to be read after the *Simchat Torah* holiday which follows after.

The Hebrew calendar, used for religious, agricultural, social and trade purposes, gave equal importance to the sun and the moon. This showed that although the sun and moon are equal, as are male and female, they are not the same. Contrary to popular belief, Judaism does not view the female as inferior to the male. Rather, she is considered a more perfect vessel for God's creative energy. Created as the container of Life, she is not obligated to keep most time-bound *mitzvot* (commandments) for she already possesses nature's secrets and cycles. One of the few time-bound obligations is to light the Sabbath candles, for only she can usher in God's Holy Time for the male. Only she can receive the Holy Light of the universe. The male must ask for it, through prayer.

This notion of male/female and giving/receiving relationship is explained well by the late Rabbi Aryeh Kaplan:

When we examine the difference between giving and receiving in terms of masculinity and feminity, we can see that the paradigm of a man is more diversified, whereas the paradigm of a woman is more unified. This becomes evident in the *Sefer Yetzirah* (The Book of Creation), which states, as mentioned, that the six days of the week, which are masculine, are the six directions pointing outward. The Sabbath, on the other hand, which is feminine, is the center point that draws all six points together. Essentially, this teaches us that when we look at ourselves in terms of our external relationships, we are looking at our masculine identity. When we look at our Self, our inner core, we are almost looking at a feminine entity.

Another important idea about the female principle is that all week long in our struggle to gain spirituality, we are on a male level. On the Sabbath, we are on a female level because we can absorb the fruits of all we have done during the week. Thus, a person could work very hard spiritually all week long, but without the Sabbath he would have no way of receiving it. This is because the Sabbath is like the final *Heh* of the Tetragrammaton. It is the hand that receives. Without the Sabbath, therefore, it is like cutting off a person's hand, preventing him from receiving spirituality. It is like working for something but never receiving it. This is why the Sabbath is of such importance in Judaism.

If you think of male and female biologically, the male is the giver; the female receives and nurtures and then gives forth much more than the man initiated. The man gives over one million sperm cells from which the woman selects only one. From her one single fertilized egg, however, she gives back a complete infant. She receives, but as part of receiving, she ends up creating and building something complete. Hence, the essence of femininity turns out to be much more complex. If masculinity is giving, femininity is receiving and completing (*Inner Space*, p. 75).

The Hebrew calendar was modified only with the appearance of the solar calendar: an extra month was inserted seven times every nineteen years to create a certain symmetry with the Gregorian calendar. So much intercalculating is necessary to maintain that symmetry that a rabbi is charged with this task. How fitting — for Judaism requires a rabbi to lead his congregants, to guide them through the very complex cycles of Time that take us through earthly time and space, enabling us to enjoy God's Holy TIME and SPACE and, in effect, to reach TIMELESS-NESS.

In short, second only to the Torah is the Hebrew calendar, the Jewish nation's most imporant document. It advises, at all times, when to do what. Historically, it brought about and continues to foster the unity of the Jewish People. Theologically, it allows each Jew to keep the Torah's 613 commandments, to follow a full year's cycle of history and time. To be more exact, this calendar captures the historical energetic force of holiness and reverence that occurred on a particular date; when we reach that date each year, that very same energetic flow comes alive again, with the very same intensity of that historical event.[22] Educationally, the calendar keeps track of each week's Torah portion, read the world over with an addendum from the Prophets. Last but not least, it offers a powerful vehicle for uniting an entire people who reside in many different nations, who speak many different languages, enabling them to remain united by an intellectual and spiritual bond from Sabbath to

Sabbath, through profane time and Holy Time.

The calendar ensures that, instead of living in isolation, each Jew (male and female) will be a part of a unique experiment: creating a binary relationship between a free society and God. This is the longest relationship of its kind in the history of Mankind.

The Link Between
Both Calendars

An additional note on the importance of examining both the Egyptian and Hebrew concepts of Time, with their respective calendars, as a linked period of Time for today's civilization.

When we look at Egyptian history in isolation, we see a people who have vanished from time, with no lasting remnant of their ways of dealing with time except for the empty shells of monuments and tombs.

However, if we look at Egyptian history and contrast it with what became of the foreign nation of slaves that built these monuments and tombs, we see that time itself can be a tool to mature the Human Species in the face of adversity. Time can force us to make the changes needed to perpetuate our growth for succeeding generations.

When viewed from this perspective, the ancient Egyptians' understanding of the two forces that governed their world, namely the sun and the moon, was neither lost in time nor buried with their mummified bodies.

Rather, that understanding and the customs stemming from it were carried out of Egypt by the people once enslaved there. Outside Egypt's borders, these ways became better and more just for all. For example, they went on to espouse the belief that both the Holy priests and their followers were subject to the laws of the moon's cycles. What the Egyptians did not do — and this made all the difference — was to unite leaders and followers into one people who lived by both forces of nature: the powerful, giving force of the sun with the hidden, receptive force of the moon. Treating time this way acknowledged a binary system that all creations live by naturally. Unfortunately, it was a tool the Egyptian elite used to divide its nation into one of masters and slaves. The first group used time to pursue a hoped-for immortality; the second saw time as a vehicle that would deliver them from their bondage to a speedy, merciful death.

This situation is well exemplified by the People of Israel's exile in Egypt. but in order to appreciate that exile and the missing link which makes a calendar, we first need to understand, both historically and conceptually, the concept of the First Born.

The Hebrew word for a family's first born son is *b'chor*. First-born status (*b'chorah*) represents nobility, honor and dignity to the family. Furthermore, according to the Ramban, each *b'chor* carries the responsibility to develop a virtuous, refined character and transmit his heritage to the next generation.[23]

In *Midrashic* sources, Adam, the first man, is called the First Born (*Bamidbar Rabbah* 4:(6)8). We can understand this application *vis-a-vis* his responsibility to develop a virtuous, refined character. But how are we to make sense of his responsibility to transmit his heritage? Adam had no parents!

This apparent paradox can be resolved by examining the relationship of body and soul. The Rabbis say that the inner soul is "a portion from God above."[24] What does this mean?

In a nutshell, Man's soul is composed of five basic parts: The Inner Spiritual Soul, the Spiritual Soul, the Intellectual Soul, the Psychological Soul and the Animal Soul. The Animal Soul is intimately joined with the body. It keeps the body alive and generates all its biological functions. This soul begins the connection between the physical body and the other, loftier souls.

Next on the hierarchy is the Psychological Soul, its bottom facet attached to the Animal Soul. This soul produces our emotions and drives, which reside in the heart. The ego is derived from the two lower souls.

Moving higher, we find the Intellectual Soul, which represents our *conscious* selves. It is here that our thinking processes and our understanding originate. Housed in the brain, the bottom facet of this soul is attached to the Psychological Soul, which dwells in our hearts. It is in this bottom facet where we sense the connection and harmony between the brain and the heart and vice versa. It is at this juncture that we have the ability to choose allegiance to the Intellectual Soul (making the Psychological Soul its subordinate), or the Animal Soul (making the Psychological and Intellectual Souls subordinate to the ego).

The fourth level up is the Spiritual Soul, which is our Higher self. In it is revealed wisdom in its essence, without symbolism or representation through a medium. The Spiritual Soul has no representation in the body, through which it can express itself. This level envelops the Intellectual Soul. This gives the Intellectual Soul the power to originate the thinking processes, expressed in the brain through symbolism and representation. This is because the brain is a medium for the expression of the Intellection Soul. And this is what we know and experience as our normal, conscious selves. The Spiritual Soul, our Higher self, is *outside* the body. In many instances, it is referred to as our "True Self."

The fifth level up is the Inner Spiritual Soul, which encompasses this hierarchy of souls, undoubtedly including the body. This level connects to the ultimate Light of God, and it is this facet of the soul that the Rabbis refer to when they say that the Inner Spiritual soul is "a portion from God above." This level is called the First Born.[25]

Now that we understand more about the relationship between body and soul, we can fathom what the Ramban meant when he said Adam's responsibility was to transmit his heritage: By making contact with his Inner Spiritual Soul, Adam acquired the royalty of first-born status, called the B'chorah. This status afforded him the potential to internalize fully the Inner Spiritual Soul.

Had Adam fulfilled his responsibility with respect to the B'chorah, that potential would have been realized. God's unity and sovereignty throughout the universe would have been dazzlingly revealed. Adam and his universe would have become perfected and whole, offering unlimited joy to both. That joy and wholeness would have resulted from Adam's linking up to his higher True Self and to the ultimate Light of God. This is the essential meaning of first-born status. Had Adam met the challenge of the B'chorah, he would have become the Messiah.[26] Unfortunately, he did not. But when the Messiah (Mashiach) will arrive, rectifying and completing what Adam did not, he will be called the B'chor, the first born of royalty (Shemot Rabbah 19:7).

Adam had to undergo the test of the Tree of Knowledge for one purpose: to determine if he would acquire the vessel (known as the royalty of the first born) for his Inner Spiritual Soul. Would he follow his own inclinations or submit completely to the will of God? The answer to that simple question would determine whether God's unity and sovereignty would be revealed or concealed in His universe. What choices confronted Adam? By choosing not to eat from the Tree of Knowledge, he would connect himself with the B'chorah, the royalty of the First Born. Consequently, a greater magnitude of God's unity and sovereignty would exist in the universe. But by choosing to eat from the Tree of Knowledge, Adam would fail to connect with his Inner Spiritual Soul, causing a concealment of God's presence. Furthermore, Adam would grow more attached to his Animal Soul, resulting in the creation of his self-centered ego. But the consequences would not end there: The soul would experience a separation of all aspects of reality from its higher spiritual components. Comparable to the concept of human ego, this separation is known in Kabbalistic writings as "the shells of concealment." It is also referred to as the "Serpent" that produces separation and concealment.[27]

From then on, the B'chorah (royalty of the first born) became hidden in the shells of concealment, meaning it would be abused selfishly by most individuals and nations. In other words, most of Adam's descendants sought royalty only to manipulate the environment and enhance their ego.

Finally, twenty generations after Adam, Abraham came along. To begin to undo the imperfection of creation, he took on Adam's failed mission: accepting the yoke of royalty of the first born (this is also the taste of the Messiah). This task is to connect physical reality to its higher spiritual counterparts.

This was no mean feat. Abraham had to accept responsibility for rectifying creation on behalf of all humanity, all of Adam's descendants. Abraham accepted this responsibility not only for himself but also for those of his descendants willing to follow his example.

Since the royalty of the first born was in a defiled state for all humanity, individuals alone could not complete this task. Furthermore, at that time this royal supremacy, the B'chorah, was embodied in its most ego-centered state by an empire that manipulated all other nations. That empire was Egypt, a world power whose might stemmed directly from its possession of the royalty of the B'chorah.

To complete Adam's mission, Abraham had to wrest the B'chorah from the Egyptian nation. No individual could battle a nation and emerge victorious. Therefore, a nation, born out of Abraham's descendants, had to take root in Egypt itself. That nation had to be subdued into slavery by Egypt while miraculously retaining their identity as Abraham's descendants. Even as slaves, this nation was able to refine their virtuous character and transmit the heritage of Abraham, Isaac and Jacob to its offspring.

For Abraham's descendants to retain their identity while enslaved required a self-control that ultimately led to dominance over the Egyptians. In effect, their persecutions under the Egyptians only paved the way for the transfer of sovereignty from the oppressor to the oppressed. And that transfer of sovereignty enabled the Hebrew nation to redeem the royalty of the First Born, the B'chorah. Before being enslaved, they only had the status of a large group of individuals; now they had acquired the status of a unified people, the national called Israel.

As a nation, the people of Israel make their exodus from Egypt, but not before the Egyptians endured ten plagues. A revelation of God's Supreme Sovereignty, these plagues empowered the nation of Israel to usurp Egypt's supremacy, including the royalty and strength of the First Born, the B'chorah, trapped heretofore by the Egyptian dynasty. Kabbalistic writings refer to that dynasty as the Great Serpent, alluded to in Ezekiel (29:3). This Great Serpent represents the concealment of God's sovereignty. In Kabbalah, this state of concealment is called "the Staff which turns into a Serpent." The Staff illustrates the dominance of God's sovereignty, while the Serpent represents the power of ego, trying to control by concealing God's sovereignty and unity. The "staff turning into a Serpent" means that God's revealed dominion becomes subdued by the Serpent for the time being - not that the Serpent is now stronger or has an independent power unto itself, God forbid! Rather, God's sovereignty and dominion rule the Serpent "behind his back," in a hidden manner. Although the Serpent may see itself as a power in its own right, in truth it is being controlled constantly by God.

But in the case where "The Serpent turns into a Staff," the "serpent power" submits itself completely to reveal God's sovereignty. A prime example of this phenomenon is the staff of Moses. When transformed into a serpent, that staff called forth God's ten plagues. In other words, the supreme power which was to reveal God's divine royalty was now released through the ten plagues, especially through the last one, the smiting of the first born. This process shattered those shells of concealment, releasing the supreme power, the B'chorah, to be expressed through the nation of Israel. This is how, through its suffering under Egyptian rule and through the Staff of Moses' response to that Egyptian rule, the nation of Israel reclaimed the B'chorah, the first born.[28]

Acquiring the first born liberated the nation of Israel from its bondage, paving the way for its transformation, forty-nine days later at Mount Sinai, into masters of creation.

The first step required for that transformation was for the nation of Israel to acquire mastery over time. This was achieved particularly through the commandment of *Kiddush Hachodesh* (sanctifying the start of each lunar month), a commandment that lay the foundation for structuring an astronomical calendar.

The Hebrew slaves' historical astronomical calendar was launched on the very night of the exodus from what was once but is no longer the Great and Mighty Egypt. Pivotal to this calendar is the *mitzvah* (commandment) of sanctifying the start of each lunar month. This was the first *mitzvah* given to the Israelites in Egypt.

The Moon, a heavenly body whose light is received from the sun, represents the receiving force, that is accepting God's emanation within the entire universe. Since the lunar year is comprised of 354 days (sometimes 355 days) it falls short of the solar year usually by eleven days. If uncorrected for two or three years, this discrepancy would cause the lunar months to coincide with inappropriate solar seasons. Since Passover must be celebrated in the spring, an extra month is added to the lunar calendar every two or three years. A year featuring this extra month (called Adar II) is called the *Shnat Ha'ibur*, meaning leap year or, literally, the gestational year.

Seven leap years occur every nineteen years to synchronize the lunar and solar cycles. This balances the sun's and moon's two patterns of time. Through this process, the sun's giving force unites with the moon's receptive force. With this "union," they "give birth" to a new emanation in the universe. This is short-lived because the 29- or 30-day lunar month will again fall short of the 30- or 31-day solar month, making the lunar year 10-11 days shorter than the solar year.

In Talmudic sources, this is called the *Sod Ha'ibur*, the secret of gestation. This secret was revealed only to select rabbis renowned for their scholarship and piety.[29] When that secret was combined with the *mitzvah* of *Kiddush Hachodesh*, the result was true mastery of time. For example, if mathematics proved that a given day was the last day of a particular month and the Rabbis of the High Court declared that day the first day of the following month, then that day would actually be the first day of the new month![30]

It is interesting to note that from the lunar perspective, there is no concept of years or even days. The concept of a 24-hour day comes from the time it takes the Earth to revolve once on its axis. Yet from the Earth's perspective, there is no concept of months or years; only days have relevance. In other words, the concept of a year exists solely *vis-a-vis* the Sun. Furthermore, the concept of a month exists solely *vis-a-vis* the Moon as it revolves around the Earth. In other words, a calendar containing days, months and years must be based on these astronomical phenomena: a rotating Earth (accounting for the days), a rotating Moon (accounting for the months) and a Sun around which our earth revolves (accounting for the year). This is the calendar which derives from the commandment of *Kiddush Hachodesh* and *Shnat Ha'ibur*. It is this calendar which simultaneously synthesizes the relationship of the Earth, the Sun and the Moon. This is a calendar based on natural astronomical phenomena, in contrast to the solar calendar, artificially divided into months that have no link to natural phenomena.

It is no coincidence that the Hebrews left Egypt on a night boasting a full moon: the 15th of Nissan, the first night of Passover. Talmudic sages state that on this wondrous night, the sun shone brightly in the moonlit sky. This was the remarkable setting for the transference of mastery of the solar and lunar cycles called *Kiddush Hachodesh*, also known as the astronomical calendar. Not that the Hebrews usurped this knowledge on their own volition; this commandment was given by God to Moses and Aaron in Egypt. The acquisition from Egypt of the *B'chorah* coupled with the Hebrews' mastery of the astronomical calendar, are the key components that gave birth to the nation of Israel on that Passover night.

When the Messiah comes, lunar and solar time will be synchronized completely. That is, lunar and solar months will contain exactly 30 days. Each year will contain 360 days, giving us a year resembling a perfect 360-degree circle with each day representing one degree.[31]

The Torah, given by God to these people 3,300 years ago at the foot of Mount Sinai, is both written and oral. The written Torah (the Five Books of Moses) can be compared to a short-hand summary of a complex system of teachings (Torah literally means teaching), but the Oral Torah (commonly defined as the Talmud) cracks that short-hand code with highly detailed information. Oral Torah was originally given to Moses at Sinai, though intentionally not in written form. It comprises the main component of the oral tradition, a scientific methodology of logic concerning laws, rituals and morality. That methodology, used throughout the Talmud, clarifies how to read the written Torah and what is hinted at in its code. Without the oral tradition, the written Torah remains a concealed book.

A second facet of the oral tradition is called the *Kabbalah*. Derived from the Hebrew word KaBeL meaning "receive," *Kabbalah* was received as part of the Sinai experience. This mystical component of the oral tradition is esoteric - concealed - whereas the first component of the oral tradition is exoteric, revealed. The *Kabbalah* reveals an added dimension to the workings of God, illuminating how the universe is run, explaining the meaning of the exoteric laws and rituals.

What is the purpose of these inner teachings found in the *Kabbalah*? To clarify unity shared by the Torah and all wisdoms, connected by the light of God. *Kabbalah* is the inner light which fills Judaism's exoteric laws, rituals and wisdom.

If we would have merited receiving God's first set of tablets at Mount Sinai, we would experience the interconnectedness of all wisdom with much greater intensity than we do today. Even our physical realities would become ethereal. We would be able to see through our hard/soft reality, like looking through glass (our reality) to see the inner workings of how everything unites within the inner light of creation. The *Midrash* calls this the Or Haganuz, the hidden light (also known as the Messianic light). Our sages explain that when the Messiah (*Mashiach*) comes, we will still have Torah and *mitzvot*, but they also will be ethereal! It is important to note that the relationship of body and soul, vessel and inner light, outer and inner, revealed and concealed, etc., will always exist. However, the unification of the contra-dictory pairs would be experienced in a profoundly different way, depending on the spiritual level of the universe at that time.

That level represents the Garden of Eden on earth. At that Messianic level, we will resume where Adam and Eve left off. If the Children of Israel had not begun to worship the golden calf, a sin which prompted Moses to shatter the first set of tablets, the Messianic era would have begun at Mount Sinai. We cannot fathom what a Messianic life is like because that mystery was contained in that first set of tablets. Not only were those tablets shattered, but the letters engraved on them were erased. In other words, the tablets' inner light was extinguished.

Unlike the first tablets, engraved by God in Heaven, the second tablets were carved out by Moses here on earth. Had the first tablets remained whole, outer reality, like the Torah itself, would be heavenly and ethereal. With the second tablet as our guide, our bodies and all of outer reality remain physical, opaque and fragmented. Hope, however, springs eternal: Despite our harsh physical reality, our evil inclinations and our lives' fragmentation, we can still purify ourselves through the light of Torah, elevating and uniting all reality until we are ready to receive the rekindled light of the first tablets. This will take place during the Messianic era.

But the Messianic era has not yet begun. Does this mean we are doomed to complete existential darkness? No! The harder we strive to master the Torah, the more its light will shine from its hiding place, purifying us and sharing with us a glimpse of the reconciliation to be found within the inner mode of the universe. It is like peeking through a keyhole at wonders that have been kept behind closed doors.

Why is a peek all we can get? All of creation - the Torah and especially the *Kabbalah* - remains concealed from human beings (except for a select few) because they must be protected from its blinding light. Humanity is simply not ready yet to witness that light at full strength.[32] Someday, men and women will become mature and stable enough to understand how to use that light. The fact that *Kabbalah* is studied so widely today suggests a spiritual renaissance that could launch the arrival of the true Messianic era.

The Messianic era will begin with a revelation that will occur during the sixth millennium and endure until the universe completes 6,000 years known as the six stages toward the creation of the perfect world. The seventh 1,000-year stage will be an era of planetary unity, referred to by Talmudic sages as "Holy Time." It will complete one entire cycle of space/time as we know it.[33] This Messianic vision, shared by many religions, will be repeated again and again through God's Timeless Time and Spaceless Space, known as the Infinite Light of God, Ein Sof.

PART II

A Study in the
Perennial Philosophy
Through Kabbalah

Introduction

During my final year of graduate studies, I realized it would be beneficial to share the ideas in my thesis (Perennial Philosophy Through *Kabbalah*) with those most likely to be affected by it, namely, educators.

I decided to take a course entitled "Frontiers of Knowledge: Integrating Concepts in Science, Religion, Art, Education and Philosophy." Although offered by the Department of Education, it seemed to be just what I needed to clarify the ideas behind my thesis.

The course's required readings filled me with enthusiasm, but soon I had second thoughts about the class's value. My focus was on philosophy and the quest for knowledge; my classmates' primary goal was communication skills. Registering for this course suddenly seemed like a big mistake. Still, I tried to keep in mind what our professor had said at the outset: The more errors we make and the faster we make them, the faster our knowledge will grow. Trying to keep an open mind, I decided to give this new principle a chance.

It was worth it. The course was just what I needed to grow and to achieve my academic goals. It helped me realize that before

I could even begin to formulate a unified theory of knowledge, I would have to clarify, refine, and possibly redefine my own position concerning the educational system that now teaches us about ourselves and the world we live in. I realized that those to be affected most by a new, radical theory of knowledge would be those in the teaching community of tomorrow. I realized that representatives of that very group were my classmates.

I began retracing and rethinking all the ideas I had focused on over the past thirteen years, trying to pinpoint the one thread they all had in common. I had to find the common denominator that would make my theory-in-formation meaningful across all disciplines. I knew deep down that it existed, but I had not yet found it.

Fortunately, one might even say fatefully, each of my classmates was engaged in a different field of study. Each had a distinct set of problems, linked to specialty and particular interests. I was determined to serve them all, to offer them a universally practical formula, enabling them to master their academic discipline without feeling isolated from the rest of us.

I placed great demands on my unified theory-in-formation. It had to be both practical and wise. It had to have the capacity to answer all concerns if it were to answer any. Once again, I contemplated Life and the disciplines established to solve its problems. I could not clump all of life's facets into one melange of information; that would eliminate the diversity of our universe. Instead, I was determined to examine each and every facet of life, much as a jeweler examines close-up the most perfectly cut diamond, noticing how each and every facet is interconnected. However, a good jeweler relies on more than his monocle. He holds the diamond at arm's length to expose it to the light, to see how it reflects the light and captures it, to reveal a brilliant explosion of color emanating from the diffusion of light by the diamond's facets. What looks like pure, colorless light becomes a rainbow of multifaceted dimensions.

The diamond became my model as I struggled to create a unified theory of knowledge, a theory that would illuminate the many facets of our academic system, a system that, in turn, is supposed to shed light on the world we live in. According to Genesis, that world does indeed have light as its first ingredient. I took that as my cue to examine each discipline, with all its richness, separately at first. But then we had to stand back, do away with our microscopes and telescopes, and see how all knowledge interconnects and forms a perfect symmetry. That symmetry will shed light on the true essence of this universe, our home.

As my search continued, I discovered that indeed every discipline I explored has a common denominator: light. Science deals with light as a property of Space and as a measure of Time. Religion deals with light not only as God's first gift to the universe, but as a symbol for the Wisdom God imparts, Wisdom that enables human beings to see God's True Essence. Philosophy deals with light as a property from the sun that lets human beings use their senses to examine their world, and then, with their brains, to try and make sense out of it. Philosophy helps us see how we relate to the world, what the world is, and what we are. This is illustrated most powerfully in Plato's allegory of the cave and the Philosopher King.

My diamond metaphor offered me much moral support as my quest for an interdisciplinary theory of knowledge continued. I was determined that, like a diamond, my theory would shed light on philosophy, science, religion, psychology, art and nature itself. I hoped my theory would unlock many mysteries. My quest brought to mind the secret of the great Pyramid of Giza, about which the esoteric teachings states, "As above, so below." For me, this has always alluded to the fact that there is an inverted pyramid right beneath the one we identify more easily. Together, these two triangles form a diamond.

And so, if science, philosophy and religion form one "triangle" of light, we also have art, psychology and nature: another "triangle" sharing that same thread of light, revealing it in a different way, much like the Yin/Yang in ourselves and in our world. The line separating light from dark and day from night in our world is so fine that sometimes it is imperceptible. A fine line also separates these six disciplines which, when viewed as a whole, will create a prism. That prism can illuminate the universe, revealing the perfect symmetry and harmony missing in today's academic (and solar) system.[34] The question is not whether they can be achieved. The question is whether they are wanted.

Perennial Philosophy Through Kabbalah

Perennial Philosophy has always been the source of Mankind's Wisdom concerning itself and its Universe. It is based on the principle that everything that exists emanates from an unknown source of Energy called Cosmic Energy by quantum physicists and God by theologians. In Kabbalistic terms, this energy is known simultaneously as "All That Is" and "No-Thing."

Most Kabbalistic teachings of the world's major religions state that this energy generated itself into forms of matter that became known as Creation. Creation took place at increasingly compli-cated levels, through a multitude of patterns that resulted in multidimensional forms of matter. One important assertion in Perennial Philosophy is that these patterns of manifestation that make up our reality were, are, and always will be the same. This assertion is the basis for the corollary that reality is of a quality and quantity that never changes. Only our perception of reality can change.[35]

Throughout the ages, the founders of higher institutions of learning have used Perennial Philosophy as the basis of all knowledge taught about ourselves and our world. And because its aim is to transform human consciousness, increasing our awareness of our purpose and connection to all that exists (including Time and Space), this philosophy always has been taught through a philosophical analysis of morals, ethics and religion.

In this fashion, academies of higher learning provided their students with a synthesis of Wisdom, knowledge and logic. This synthesis helped students understand the diverse nature of subjects they were being taught. It also helped them become more perceptive of their world, enabling them to contribute as adults to a better future.

Today's universities should teach Perennial Philosophy in a universally acceptable manner, for today's students stand at a crossroad that separates one generation — and one century — from another. Young minds the world over are contemplating old and new, war and peace, good and evil. Students are witnessing near-universal doubt about our planet. Like us, they wonder: will that planet survive as one of civilized and united nations, or will it succumb to insanity and utter destruction?

Standing at a similar crossroad over 200 years ago, America's founding fathers used the Wisdom of Perennial Philosophy to create the United States. Almost 2,000 years ago, Jesus of Nazareth stood at a different crossroad and, through Perennial Philosophy, taught Mankind how to create a better future through an Illumination of Faith.[36] Over 3,500 years ago, Moses had a similar opportunity to give an entire people the essence of Perennial Philosophy in the form of Ten Commandments.

Socrates used Perennial Philosophy to teach a new way to question and discover Truth. Michelangelo and Leonardo da Vinci used Perennial Philosophy to give civilization a new way to view itself. And in the twentieth century, a man named Albert Einstein stood at civilization's most awesome crossroad and, with the tools of Perennial Philosophy, found a totally new way to view Time and Space. In the process, he gave Mankind a completely altered Universe to live in.

These are only some of the giants who understood Perennial

Philosophy well enough to recognize that crossroads do exist, and that they must be used to the fullest to benefit Mankind and its planet.

The question facing mankind today is: Can the planet's academic institutions rise above their political differences and create a universally acceptable Perennial Philosophy? If the answer is yes, those students with a mission to build bridges between peoples and nations actually will create a unified and harmonious twenty-first century.

The world's political leaders seem uniformly pessimistic about achieving international unity. However, the world's students by and large espouse a different consensus. They display a special unity through the clothes they wear, the music they enjoy and the causes they champion, particularly the quest for global peace and ecological safety.

Today's under-thirty generation shares a strong curiosity about ancient esoteric teachings, only available until recently to members of secret fraternal organizations. These brotherhoods may have had different cultural symbols, languages and philosophies. Originating from East or West, they nevertheless were teaching the same Truth. This became evident since the 1980's, when young people began to travel more than ever, intermingling with their overseas counterparts. As they began reading newly translated esoteric doctrines of both East and West, these young people realized that their academic institutions had denied them these invaluable teachings, teachings that could enable them to make sense of the global mess facing them.

The students sought out those unique academicians who had the vision to bring Perennial Philosophy into the classroom. In the process, academic administrators were forced to realize just how criminal it was to relegate these teachings to the bookshelves of theology departments. Visionary administrators acknowledged that education as a whole had suffered great injustice when the eternal religious truths of past civilizations were separated from the philosophical disciplines that subsequently helped mankind understand these Truths.

Student frustration sparked this administrative shift. New Age books were being sold on campus as fast as they came off the printing press. Unfortunately, many students in search of ultimate Truth have fallen prey to any author claiming to be "New Age." Many authors base their books on Perennial Philosophy but are unable to guide their readers through such difficult material and to its hidden messages. Students need a disciplined system, within university walls, to help them separate the wheat from the chaff as they strive to glean the Wisdom of the ages.

One need not look far to see that our educational systems have been victimized over the last twenty years by the world's major sociological crises. The three R's were abandoned. Logic — both as skill and syllabus — was deemed irrelevant. Instead, school administrators were convinced that science alone would ensure student success. Obviously they never envisioned a time when people would complete four years of college and remain unable to tally a simple grocery bill without a calculator.

Most of today's college students express anger at their parents' generation for greedily destroying our planet's ozone layer; for poisoning the crops that ended up on their dinner table; for polluting the waters that ultimately streamed into their kitchen sinks; and for sullying the very air that entered their children's lungs. These young people want to get back to basics: Truth and Justice. However, they feel forced to compromise their beliefs to get a good job and simply survive.

Among these disenchanted people are my son and daughter. During and after their college years, I would overhear them discussing with friends the state of the planet and the human race. Their criticisms were many, but these two resurfaced most frequently: Governments around the world toppled, leaving poverty in their wake, while our own elected officials allowed this economic collapse to fortify our financial clout. And scientists peered into microscopes and telescopes to answer Life's problems, yet admitted they did not know the cause of creation.

New Age lecturers attracted this disenchanted group world-wide. When they asserted that the scientific community would never find the source of Creation because that source could never be seen through a telescope or a microscope, these young people sat up, took note — and took notes! They heard New Age gurus state that the creative intelligence that brought everything into existence cannot be seen, but can be perceived through Perennial Philosophy. The New Age leaders attempted to convince college students that what they were seeking could not be found in an academic setting. Sadly, many young people believed this and left their university to follow a guru and become "enlightened."

This particular population rapidly lost respect for parents, teachers, knowledge and even morality. America's educational system was becoming a shadow of its former self. Sexual promiscuity among teens and pre-teens was commonplace. Drug abuse was taking its toll on adults, adolescents and children. As this century draws to a close, we witness the tragic results of this decadence: the AIDS epidemic.

In the eyes of my children and their friends, many institutions were responsible for society's decline. But, as they saw it, the academic community deserved most of the blame.

Its fatal error: channeling all of its resources toward the creation of a sophisticated and scientific world. In contrast, academicians of Eastern cultures balanced new ideas with the Perennial Philosophy that had always been the backbone of academia. Chinese and Japanese universities still offer a solid philosophy curriculum for all students, simply adding more course requirements for those majoring in science or math.

America's academic community chose a different route. It decided to forego Perennial Wisdom in favor of all that was new and scientific. Perhaps it should have paid closer attention to Werner Von Braun, who said, as we entered the Space Age, that science and religion are like sisters, walking hand in hand. Their basic truths, he said, not only help explain one another, but ultimately boil down to the same thing. Anyone familiar with Perennial Philosophy would agree that Von Braun was drawing two conclusions: science and religion are two distinct ways to penetrate Perennial Philosophy. Both disciplines should be taught in institutes and academies of higher learning.

The New Age books that captivated young adults everywhere could have been required reading for college courses, courses that could have shed light on the confusion students face daily. In a world lacking moral guidelines, these young people need a universal philosophy to guide them to a new century.

Facing this generation is the formidable task of fusing our technological scientific advances to ensure our planet's survival. But this is a generation for whom science and technology is not enough. This is a generation that refuses to abandon the beauty of nature or the sound of music. This is a generation that needs Perennial Philosophy, for its wisdom conveys the purpose of Humanity's Soul.

We need all the Wisdom we can get. Authentic Perennial Philosophy must counteract the distortion of its teachings perpetuated by many Third World nations. That distortion promotes fundamentalism and Western Civilization's total destruction.

Small doses of Perennial Philosophy have been injected into college curricula. But most New Age philosophers believe it is hardly enough. They want college campuses to become the forum for enlightenment, without crystals, Ouija boards or Tarot cards. They maintain that if Perennial Philosophy were taught in a way that would expose all its hidden aspects, students would see that all the trappings associated with the New Age lifestyle (e.g., crystals, Tarot cards and meditation) have their roots in Perennial Philosophy.

This volume examines Perennial Philosophy through the eyes of *Kabbalah* because all esoteric writers acknowledge that Jewish mysticism is the foundation for all esoteric teachings. It was inspired by an education course I took in 1988, entitled "Frontiers of Knowledge: Integrating Concepts in Science, Religion, Art, Education, Sociology and Philosophy." My classmates were certified teachers seeking innovative instruction techniques. Nevertheless, many resisted the course's radical premise that, no matter what the subject, teachers will enhance learning if they integrate other disciplines into their curriculum.

When I mentioned that my goal was to formulate a unified theory of knowledge, a binding force for all disciplines, my classmates seemed terribly bothered. They voiced concern that such an approach to teaching would divest their individual disciplines of academic autonomy.

Their fear reminded me of Christian theologian Johann Von Meyer's German preface to the Kabbalah's *Sefer Yetzirah* (The Book of Creation). Although published in 1830, his words express ideas found in many recently published books, books that would have allayed my classmates' fears.

Dr. Von Meyer states:

> This book is for two reasons highly important: in the first place, that the real *Kabbalah*, or mystical doctrine of the Jews, which must be carefully distinguished from its excrescences, is in close connection and perfect accord with the Old and New Testaments; and in the second place, that the knowledge of it is of great importance to the philosophical inquirers, and cannot be put aside. Like a cloud permeated by beams of light which makes one infer that there is more light behind it, so do the contents of this book, enveloped in obscurity, abound in coruscations of thought, reveal to the mind that there is a still more effulgent light lurking somewhere, and thus inviting us to further contemplation and investigation, and at the same time, demonstrating the danger of a superficial investigation, which is so prevalent in modern times, reflecting that which cannot be understood at first sight.

These words make me wonder: How many books delineating the different forms of Perennial Philosophy are sitting on bookshelves, gathering dust? Books like these could shed old light on new problems and new light on old problems, proving that there is nothing new under the sun except our perceptions.

Contemporary philosophers and Kabbalists are well aware of the problems that repeatedly plague Mankind. The late scholar, rabbi, and Kabbalist, Aryeh Kaplan, introduced his *Meditations and Kabbalah* with the following:

It is with great trepidation that one begins to write a book such as this, involving some of the most hidden mysteries of the *Kabbalah*. Many would question the Wisdom and propriety of placing such information in a printed book, especially in an English translation. But so much misinformation has already been published that it is virtually imperative that an authentic, authoritative account be published. It is for this reason, as well as other reasons which I am bound by an oath to conceal, that the great living masters of *Kabbalah* have voiced their approval that such a book be published.

Having read the complementary words of two such distinguished thinkers, I grew more determined to teach a Unified Theory of Perennial Philosophy to our young people. But I wanted to do this responsibly, in a structured setting like the university. I wanted to dispel the many myths, sold in underground stores and espoused by New Age cults, about the true meaning of Perennial Philosophy for today's world.

My first goal was to redefine the term "Perennial Philosophy" so that the fear it evoked would be alleviated. I wanted academicians and students alike to see that my unified theory was, in fact, not new at all. It was merely a newly presented form of Perennial Philosophy, a philosophy that over many centuries had been called by many different names, but that in essence offered the same synthesis of knowledge and wisdom.

I wanted my thesis to be theoretical and practical, simple despite its broad scope. In short, I saw it as academic bookends, holding a multitude of knowledge within a framework of form, interrelatedness and harmony.

This metaphor reflects the essence of *Kabbalah*, for *Kabbalah* talks of a balance and harmony within creation that incorporates planets, moons, suns, life, atmosphere, Time/Space, energy, numbers, letters, patterns of emanation, and whatever these entities emanated from called "The Cause of All Causes."

Science has for many years tried to find this cause, but had to concede that whatever it is, it cannot be seen through telescopes or microscopes. This Creative Intelligence is a *oneness of multiplicity that operates in perfect harmony, synchronicity, balance, and rhythm, and we are a part of it all.* This concept is taught through Perennial Philosophy, with a multitude of different symbols, metaphors and allegories, depending on the underlying religious or esoteric teaching being used.

In the past (and even today in some religions), esoteric schools were part of a mystical brotherhood that based its teachings on esoteric material at the core of the religion it represented. The brotherhood would use this material to formulate its essential teachings, known as its Perennial Philosophy.

While these many philosophies might have seemed different to both unenlightened observers and actual adherents, truly enlightened leaders knew that these philosophies were merely different ways of explaining the same Truth. They differed simply because they addressed populations with different languages, different cultures, different needs and different societies. Sometimes, a leader would create a different version to maintain power and manipulate the masses.

What began as a Primordial teaching, handed down orally from one generation to another, created by the Cosmic Consciousness of a handful of highly enlightened and spiritually pure beings, sadly became diverse philosophies lacking a unified Perennial version.

But religions and brotherhoods are not the only culprits in this perpetration of fraud against Mankind. Science has done its share, cleverly manipulating the minds of the masses, insisting that there was no creation of Man/Woman but, rather, that humans evolved from other species.

How sad and ironic that Charles Darwin, the scientist most responsible for this belief, never took the time to study the ancient texts of the Perennial Philosophies, especially those of *Kabbalah*. If he had, he would have seen that while, on the surface, religion does assert that all of life was created by an intelligent, wise and omnipotent Creator, it also maintains that life emanated downwards in a spiral of energy that, in turn, created a cosmology consisting of a multi-level reality. Each level represented a higher one. In other words, each level represented a form of matter and a state of being more advanced than its predecessor, until what we call life was ready to manifest itself in its simplest form. Eventually, according to Kabbalah, increasingly more complicated emanations of Life Energy manifested themselves, in accord with a divine, Intelligent Will. At this point, Kabbalah speaks of a Creative Intelligence eliciting the spiritual energy of "Soul" to enable the species of Man/Woman to come into being.

Perhaps this is what Darwin was trying to grasp when, perhaps unsuccessfully, he formulated his Theory of Evolution.

Unfortunately, he misunderstood the essence of creation: that it is constantly evolving (in time) and unfolding (in space).[37]

The Kabbalah's interpretation of creation certainly mirrors science's image of DNA. Simultaneously, it clarifies how only 23 chromosomes can create the infinite multitude of men and women whose facial features, skin color, hair, height, intelligence and talents (to name only a few attributes) differ. Through Kabbalah, one understands this as being a joining of two trees of life (male/female) (Adam/Eve) with the Creator as the twenty-third unit.

(11 + 11) (11 + 11)

According to Rabbi Yehuda Ashlag, who authored the only complete translation of the Zohar (one of the major books within Kabbalah), "the Creative Intelligence is Wisdom, and this Wisdom is no more and no less than the order of roots which concentrate according to the laws of cause and effect." They do so, he said, according to absolute fixed rules. They combine and hit the target of a single supernal purpose called "the revelation of His Goodness to His creatures in the world."

Rabbi Ashlag states that this pertains to both Mankind as a whole and individuals and creatures as specific entities, and that in the end, all of Mankind must come to the same development as the specific individual throughout history, who did it sooner.

"How then," states Rabbi Ashlag, "can one account for the multitude of countenances and '*Sefirot*' (levels), within creation, if the only purpose is for the human soul to find God consciousness? The answer, according to *Kabbalah*, lies in nature itself."

Biologists tell us that even the smallest of creatures contains millions of capillaries and veins visible to the human eye. Scientists have confirmed that these creatures have tens of millions of additional blood vessels invisible to the human eye. How many combinations and channels must there be within nature's intelligent, creative environment to allow for such diversity? If one views the creative process according to Kabbalistic teachings, this process of uninterrupted diversity has its roots in the emanation of Primordial Creative Energy.

Kabbalah explains that the creative process rests on the cosmological emanation of an energy so powerful that it creates existence out of a void. These emanations of energy unfolded in progressive degrees of power that resulted in Ten Primordial Frequencies that are parts, so to speak, of one. This is always referred to as "The Tree of Life." In *Kabbalah*, these ten emanations of existence took the form of the numbers zero through nine.

These ten, in turn, manifested themselves into all of creation, through 22 less powerful levels of energy, that could then be combined in an unrelenting multitude of combinations of creation, and thus matter, and finally reality as we know it in its many different forms. In *Kabbalah*, these 22 levels of energy took the form of the 22 letters of the Hebrew alphabet.

If one looks at the 22 chromosomes found in DNA, plus its one sex chromosome, and compares it with the 22 emanations and one Tree of Life, one can't help but wonder how the Kabbalists of old could possibly have concocted the same numbers of creation as did twentieth century scientists.[38]

Furthermore, *Kabbalah* states that these emanations take place on four levels called "The Four Worlds." The emanations' energy flows down through these four worlds in a polarity that is dual in nature. This polarity is called the masculine and feminine, a principle very much aligned with that of Yin/Yang in the Tao Te Ching teachings of ancient China. Keep in mind that the Tao is the Chinese version of the Tree of Life, and both teachings represent different forms of Perennial Philosophy. Furthermore, Kabbalistic principles are mirrored in quantum physics and mathematics, where we find the ten number base and acknowledgement that although no cause can be found for the origin of the universe, nothing can appear in the physical realm out of nothing, without violating physical laws. As Paul Davies states in *The Cosmic Blueprint*, "How can something come into existence uncaused?"

An increasing number of scientists and writers have come to realize that the physical world's ability to organize itself consti-tutes a fundamental and mysterious property of the universe. The fact that nature as Creative Power can produce progressively richer varieties of complex entities challenges the very founda-tion of contemporary science.

"The greatest riddle of cosmology," writes philosopher Karl Popper, "may well be ... that the universe is, in a sense, creative."

Belgian physicist and Nobel Laureate Ilya Prigogine, who co-authored with Isabelle Stengers *Order Out of Chaos: Man's New Dialogue with Nature* (1984), reached similar conclusions when he stated, "Our universe has a pluralistic, complex character. Structures may disappear, but they also may appear." Prigogine and Stengers, whose book was inspired by the work of Erich Jantsch, state that, like them, Jantsch asserts that nature has a "free will" of sorts and thus is capable of generating novelty. They quote Jantsch: "We may one day perhaps understand the self-organizing process of a universe which is not determined by the blind selection of initial conditions, but has the potential of partial self-determination."

It seems that quantum physicists are beginning to grasp what Perennial Philosophy (and its major source, *Kabbalah*) has taught all along, especially when one reads Paul Davies's *The Cosmic Blueprint*. In it, he acknowledges that scientists are now paying more attention to the problem of the Origin of the Universe. In fact, the central question of Dr. Davies's book is: What is the source of the universe's creative potency? Interestingly, he didn't have to go past one of his initial paragraphs to find his answer: "To most people it is obvious that the universe forms a coherent whole. We recognize that there are a great many components that go together to make up the totality of existence, but they seem to hang together, if not in cooperation, then at least in peaceful coexistence. In short, we find order, unity and harmony in nature where there might have been discord and chaos" (p. 6).

These words affirm that Perennial Philosophy is needed today more than ever before. It can lend practical insight to confusing scientific theories that cannot be proven in the laboratory. And, if taught logically to today's youth, this practical insight might be the key they need to integrate their technological, sterile environment with their latent spirituality, a spirituality that links them to a higher creative power. If young people were shown that *Aleph*, the first letter of the Hebrew alphabet and the first of the 22 physical emanations of the creative power, is almost identical to the encircled Ying/Yang symbol, they would probably see the link between all forms of Perennial Philosophy.

As Spanish Kabbalist Carlo Suarez states in his study of the *Sefer Yetzirah*, "*Kabbalah* is indeed a science and the *Sefer Yetzirah* (The Book of Creation), a precise and accurate treatise on the structure of cosmic energy, written in a hidden code that even the greatest of post-Kabbalists were not completely aware of, due to the fact that only recently has Mankind's historical evolution developed the brain's so-called 'objective' powers of thought." This may be one more philosophical explanation of Darwin's theory of evolution, a time-tested explanation that clarifies both the manifestations of evolution and, more importantly, the hidden reasons for that manifestation.

In its many forms, Perennial Philosophy has withstood the test of Time, merging in our day as a guiding light to help Humanity find its true essence. Research reveals that there always were esoteric associations that bound together men and women of good faith, individuals who preserved and perpetuated the One and Only True Perennial Philosophy of the Divine Mysteries of Creation, until Mankind was mature enough in academic knowledge, and comprised of enough "Seekers of the Path" to allow this hidden knowledge to come into the light.

With each succeeding generation, members of fraternal orders had to increase their knowledge of Truth and Wisdom. They had to learn how to walk that very narrow "Middle Path." Once they reached these milestones, they were worthy of being called "Twice Born," for they had been born a second time out of the "Womb of Wisdom."

These men and women were sworn to secrecy to prevent their powerful knowledge about creation to fall into the wrong hands. Today, sadly, this knowledge is being used corruptly by madmen capable of destroying all life on this planet. That is why most fraternal orders have given their members the go-ahead to reveal this knowledge to all Mankind, with the hope that good will and sanity will prevail over the evil and madness in our world.

In 1912, the highly respected, non-sectarian Hermetic Order released their teachings on a limited basis. Its members foresaw evil unfolding, leading to the unspeakable evils of Hitler and the atomic bomb. In other words, its members foresaw the end of Mankind's innocence. Metaphorically, Mankind had eaten of the Tree of Life and had to leave the Garden of Eden.[39] Lacking the proper tools to create a positive world, humanity had to wander through the maze of trial and error, suffering until it could figure out how to create matter that could destroy. But as for the creation of Life, humanity was still in the dark. Even though it could create matter, it could not breathe Life into that matter.

The Hermetic Society published seven basic principles of Hermetic Philosophy. Written by Three Initiates, this small book asserts that the Society's founder, Hermes Trismegistus, was a contemporary of Abraham, said to be the first of the Hebrews to receive *Kabbalah*. He did so, they maintain, through a mystical revelation. The authors also claim that Abraham acquired a great portion of the Perennial Tradition from Hermes himself, who they believe was a physical manifestation of the biblical personage known as Enoch.

The seven Hermetic Principles, so closely bound to the Tree of Life and thus the essence of *Kabbalah*, are almost identical to the Seven Perennial Principles of Truth. The Kybalion (the title of the Hermetic principles) does this less theologically than the Kabbalistic texts. To this day, it remains one of the main vehicles for teaching Perennial Philosophy. It defines the seven principles as follows:

1) "The Principle of Mentalism:" The All is Mind; The Universe is Mental.

2) "The Principle of Correspondence:" As above, so below; As below, so above.

3) "The Principle of Vibration:" Nothing rests; Everything moves; Everything vibrates.

4) "The Principle of Polarity:" Everything is dual; Everything has poles; Everything has its pair of opposites; Like and unlike are the same; Opposites are identical in nature, but different in degree; Extremes meet; All truths are but half-truths; All paradoxes may be reconciled.

5) "The Principle of Rhythm:" Everything flows out and in; Everything has its tides; All things rise and fall; The Pendulum swing manifests in everything; The Measure of the swing to the right is the measure of the swing to the left; Rhythm compensates.

6) "The Principle of Cause and Effect:" Everything has its cause and effect; Every effect has its cause; Every cause has its effect; Everything happens according to Law; Chance is but a name for law not recognized; There are many planes of Causation, but nothing escapes the law.

7) "The Principle of Gender:" Gender is in everything;

Everything has its Masculine and Feminine Principles; Gender manifests on all planes.

It seems unlikely that any scientist would repudiate the above principles, but then neither would any Kabbalist. On the contrary, the Kabbalist would say that this is what all religions transmit esoterically to create the exoteric body of its beliefs.

In his book *Tree of Life*, contemporary British Kabbalist Z'ev ben Shimon Halevi writes: "In *Kabbalah*, the Tree of Life is a metaphoric symbol of the universe, with the creative energies flowing down to the lowest world and back up again. In this Rhythmic, Circular, and Spiral flow are contained all the laws of the universe."

Halevi explains that the relative universe hovers between two poles which are, The All (positive) and No-Thing (negative). Either end of this constantly fluctuating axis can be an entry and exit for this energy. This is because "The Tree" has two opposing pillars, with a middle pillar balancing the two, to assemble on both ends in the shape of two triangles.

The *Kabbalah* teaches that whoever can walk the Tree of Life's middle pillar becomes a true Master, balancing Life in Truth and Wisdom. Such an individual has become a Path towards Perfection for others to follow.

The Dhammapada, *Kabbalah*'s Buddhist counterpart, attempts to convey the same lesson. In his introduction to The Dhammapada, Juan Mascaro explains that the word Dharma comes from the Sanskrit root DHR, meaning to carry or support a moral or spiritual law of righteousness, The Eternal Law of the Universe, Truth. Thus, the Dhammapada is the right path of Light, which will lead us to supreme Truth, Light and Nirvana. He calls this "The Path of Perfection."

In this context, one can understand the Buddha's "Middle Path" as a narrow path of Perfection, leading to the top of the mountain. On the right is that which is too earthly and thus "Negative." On the left is that which is too heavenly and thus "Positive." These paths could be compared to the right, left and middle paths of the *Kabbalah*'s Tree of Life.

As the Bhagavad Gita states: "In the center there is the narrow path that leads to the top of the mountain. A path that suggests harmony in life. Not for one who eats too little, or too much, or sleeps too little, or too much. It is a path of Perfection" (Gita 6:16).

In short, every Perennial Tradition has sought to help its student achieve the path towards Perfection through the realization of Truth.

According to Mascaro, it was Truth, not Perfection, that all great men of contemplation sought. That One Truth was called *Tao, Allah, Aum, Brahman, Atman* or *Elohim*. And in the end, that One Truth was always the Perennial Philosophy of All That Is, being part of the One Truth. These are all fragments which fell out of the Tree of Knowledge of Supernal Wisdom.

In his introduction to Frithjof Schuon's *Transcendental Unity of Religions*, Huston Smith asserts that Perennial Truth or Philosophy is indeed the Transcendental Unity of all religions. It is their very essence. According to Smith, our age demands that religions be treated in global terms. Such a sentiment mirrors that of other Kabbalists cited in this study. However, Smith is alone in his opinion that "Transcendent Truth," the underlying factor in the metaphysical unity of religions, is accessible to very few. He believes that many look towards the exoteric, while the Truth lies in the esoteric.

While each author cited here has sought esoteric Truth on differing paths, each agrees that we must find a way to transmit these esoteric Truths worldwide, especially to our younger generation. Only then can we repair a world so damaged by pure science and technology.

Contemporary Kabbalists such as Phillip S. Berg, Z'ev ben Shimon Halevi, Yehuda Ashlag, Aryeh Kaplan, Adin Steinsaltz, as well as all Hermeticists, would certainly concur with Smith's analysis but would disagree with his prescription. These Kabbalists' assessment is almost identical to that of Ruth Nanda Anshen. In her epilogue to Paul Tillich's *Dynamics of Faith*, Anshen states that Man is developing a new consciousness which, in spite of his spiritual and moral complexity, can eventually lift the human race above and beyond its fear, ignorance and isolation. She explains that Mankind is awakening to the reality that science alone does not hold the answers for Mankind's ills, that we need a greater vision of humanity in a unified and peaceful world, a vision that can only be realized through expanded awareness and enlightenment.

Perhaps Smith does not share the negative viewpoint that he attributes to Frithjof Schuon. If so, he should have given the reader a positive path to follow in order to gain access to the esoteric Truth that Schuon feels is a privilege only a few can enjoy.

This positive path can be one of many, but the initial vision and impetus is always the same, agreed upon by all who have followed it. It lies in a "receiving" of a divine flash of light that comes as a result of stretching the mind's boundaries so that one can contact the primordial waves of creative energy. This "Receiving" is the system of *Kabbalah*, which has its origin in the word *lekabel*. And *lekabel* means, literally, to receive.[40]

Logic dictates that we can only attain the Primordial Traditions of Civilization, that is, Perennial Truths, through the "Wisdom" that is "Received" from the "Source." That is why *Kabbalah* seems the most logical system for extrapolating answers for today's generation.

In *The Turning Point*, Fritjof Capra assesses our highly developed scientific environment. He quotes from the *I Ching*: "After a time of decay comes the turning point. The primordial light which has been banished returns. There is movement, but it is not brought about by force ... The movement is natural, arising spontaneously. For the transformation becomes easy. The aid is discarded and the new introduced. Both measures accord with the time: Therefore, no harm results."

These sentiments were voiced repeatedly throughout the 1980's. In *Up From Eden* (1981), Ken Wilbur asserted that we had entered a "New Age" that necessitated a more unified view of humanity. The human race, he predicted, would continue to grow as a cohesive species, in tune with itself and its environment. Fortunately, Wilbur was not the only visionary reminding us that we had been destroying the only home we have. Gregory Bateson and other environmentalists had been doing that for over twenty years. And this awareness showed how important it was for ecologists, anthropologists, architects, economists, politicians and other leading forces within society to join forces, undoing the damage heaped on our society and environment, creating greater harmony and sanity in what is fast becoming an insane world.[41]

Israeli archaeologists concluded recently that to assess what kind of society they were unearthing, they had to recruit an interdisciplinary team of experts, relying on more than the limited knowledge of archaeologists. If that be true of the recreation of the past, how much more so for the creation of the future? As Kabbalist Z'ev ben Shimon Halevi explains, in all that exists there are always two aspects - the seen and the hidden. In the secular world, the seen is explored through the arts, exact fields of law and economics, sociology, politics and other disciplines analyzing human behavior. But there is no study of the unseen other than the many esoteric, occult teachings that have emerged over the past twenty years.

In religion, the seen is manifested by ritual, scriptures and services, while the hidden must bear the Light that illuminates all that is seen.

In Judaism, these hidden teachings are called *Kabbalah*. It is said to have originated with the angels, instructed by God to transmit it to Mankind. They first handed *Kabbalah* down to Adam, then to Enoch, Noah, Abraham, Isaac, Jacob, Joseph, Moses, Aaron and subsequently to Israel's kings and prophets. Moses was the only mortal to have been instructed by God alone. His task was to hand these hidden secrets of the Universe, in the form of a blueprint called Torah, to a chosen nation charged with the mission of safeguarding these secrets for future generations.

The French Kabbalist Adolphe Frank concurs with Judaic lore when he states that the *Kabbalah* was brought down from heaven, by Angels, to the first Man (ADAM - Male/Female) after the fall, in order to assist Man in regaining nobility and bliss.

Unfortunately, over the ages, many intelligent, educated and well meaning people became so caught up in the web of science that they even forgot how to ask the questions that would lead them towards Perennial Philosophy. In the interim, well meaning educators led us closer to new technologies and further away from such great philosophical minds as Moses, Wittgenstein, Cicero, Hobbs, Leibniz, Hegel, Descartes, Plato, Socrates, St. Thomas Aquinas, Buddha, Confucius, Lucretius, Jesus, Pythagoras, Heraclitus, Democritus, Plotinus, Sir Francis Bacon, Shakespeare, Michelangelo, Leonardo da Vinci, and of course Albert Einstein, who admitted to being a mystic, whose ultimate goal was to find a Unified Field Theory. Einstein was one of the few people who believed he could prove God scientifically. What a shame that the masses, led towards Freudian and Jungian analysis by scientific revolutionaries convinced that all our problems were in our mind, never knew that Freud and Jung were members of a well known Kabbalistic group. In fact, both men's theories were influenced by the many Kabbalistic texts to which they had access.

Kabbalah has also been the foundation for astrology. In *The Astrological Secrets of The Hebrew Sages*, Rabbi Joel C. Dobin writes that, when understood properly, *Kabbalah* sheds light on the twelve astrological signs. Specifically, they symbolize the twelve tribes of Israel, which in turn are symbolic of the twelve hours of day and of night that comprise a perfectly aligned day, when our planet's axis is at perfect polarity. This would take place at the Vernal Equinox (the first day of Spring, which is really the beginning of the organic year) and at the Autumnal Equinox (marking the end of Nature's yearly cycle).

Given how much we don't know about the true nature of our universe, it is not surprising that so many writers are trying to help humanity find its way back to nature. As Dr. Phillip Berg, Dean of the Research Center of *Kabbalah* in Israel and the United States, states, "The reason people in this generation seem to be so confused, lonely, depressed, frustrated and out of control of their own lives, is because they are not really aware of the forces of the Cosmos that affect us all. They are also unaware of how they affect our lives, and must learn to know the causes of creation to be able to cope with its effects."

In *The Kabbalah Connection*, Berg states that *Kabbalah* is no more arcane than chemistry, physics, music, art, mathematics, geometry or quantum mechanics. Rather, he argues convincingly, that *Kabbalah* is all of the above and much more: It is the powerful knowledge that must be taught to all who wish to be not merely educated, but illuminated with the Truth that today's generation seems so hungry for. Berg adds that writers like Carlos Castaneda, Gurdieff and De Ropp were not even aware that their writings were rooted in *Kabbalah*. He states unequivocally, "Truth is Truth, whatever hand lifts its banner, but only the Kabbalist knows its source." Berg concludes with the ironic fact that The *Kabbalah* of Creation, the Jewish people's greatest and most forgotten gift, should have become the most avidly pursued goal of the awakening non-Jew seeking enlightenment. After all, *Kabbalah* is the metaphysical transferral of energy that cannot be seen or measured until grounded in matter.

Some of the examples of this grounding are television airwaves, X-rays, radio frequencies, electricity and magnetic fields or, as Einstein preferred to call them, electromagnetic forces, forces that he believed existed as a duality, just like Time/Space. Einstein's last goal, as stated before, was to prove his Unified Field Theory. Like *Kabbalah*, it spoke of nature's Harmony and Uniformity. Furthermore, it looked for a single edifice of physical laws that could encompass all the laws of inner and outer space.

If his Unified Field Theory is proven someday, we will witness Einstein's insight that the composition and structure of all matter stems from a single cause. This would be a philosophical triumph, unifying science with the Perennial Truths taught throughout the ages by great sages the world over.

Lincoln Barnett concludes his book on Einstein by stating, "The philosophers and mystics, as well as the scientists, have always sought through their various disciplines, an introspection to arrive at a knowledge of the ultimate immutable essence that undergirds the mutable illusory world. More than 2300 years ago, Plato declared, 'The True lover of Knowledge is always striving after being ... He will not rest at those multitudinous phenomena whose existence is appearance only.'"

To that one must add that Einstein also asserted that the only world man can truly know is the world created for him by his senses.

That is what *Kabbalah* teaches as well. It teaches us that we become "Enlightened" only when we realize that EIN, that which is not, as well as the EIN-SOF (Alpha-Omega), the One that *is with no end, are simply polarities of one and the same Absolute All.* That is taught in the Hermetic Philosophy as the Principle of Polarity and in the Tao as Ying/Yang. Perhaps that is what Hegel meant by his cryptic remark, "Pure Being and Nothing are the Same."[42]

Our goal is to weave this study's many facets into a functional and practical whole, similar to the multifaceted diamond, exposing the many colors comprising the light that we see as colorless.

It would be gratifying to entertain the notion that a universal understanding of life's problems exists, but that it is a multifaceted system that cannot be found in any one discipline or religion. This system, the sum total of all the Perennial Philosophies of Man, would entertain the notion of "exposing the problem to the Light" in order to see its many facets. It would then incorporate the tools of Science, Religion, Philosophy, Psychology, Art and Nature Herself to solve the problems of humankind.

Perhaps this is the secret of the Great Pyramid of Giza: The Esoteric teachings of all the Perennial Philosophies include the axiom, "As Above, So Below and As Below, So Above." I believe this alludes to the allegorical, inverted pyramid right beneath the Great Pyramid of Giza. These two triangles do indeed form a diamond. For when one looks at the pyramid from any angle one can only see a triangle.

If Science, Philosophy and Religion share a thread of Light

through their facets of information, then Art, Psychology and Nature share that same thread by revealing how that light functions through a duality that is the Yin/Yang of ourselves and the world around us. It is a world where the fine line separating light from dark, and day from night, is so fine as to be at times imperceptible.

These merging disciplines will have to create a prism so bright that it will illuminate the universe, exposing the perfect symmetry, harmony and brilliance that can belong to the human race. The question is not whether or not it can be achieved, *but whether or not it is wanted.*

I conclude this study with a parable from the Chandgya-Upanishad:

A father said to his son, "Put some salt in water and bring it to me tomorrow morning." The son obeyed and on the following morning the father said, "Show me the salt which you put in the water last night." Of course, this was impossible to do for by dissolving, the salt had become one with the water.

"Place your tongue on the water's surface," said the father. "How does it taste?"

"It is salty," replied the son.

"Now pour off the top and drink from the center. Is it different?" asked the father.

"Still, my father, it is salty."

The father smiled wisely, and said, "Cast the water upon the ground, then return to me."

Once again the son obeyed but the salt, interpenetrating the earth with the water was not lost, for salt is eternal.

The father explained the lesson to his son saying: "Similarly, my son, the True Self of Wisdom is within your body, interpenetrating it, but you are as yet unaware of it. All who perceive a 'Self partake of this subtle essence. It is the 'True Self of All,' and, Svetaketu, you are it."

PART III

Eshet Chayil

A WOMAN OF VALOR
FOR THE
TWENTY–FIRST CENTURY

Eshet Chayil

An Accomplished Woman
(A Woman of Valor)

A woman of valor, who can find? Far beyond pearls is her
value.
Her husband's heart trusts in her and he shall lack no fortune.
She repays his good, but never his harm, all the days of her life.
She seeks out wool and linen, and her hands work willingly,
She is like a merchant's ships; from afar she brings her sustenance.
She rises while it is still nighttime, and gives food to her household
    and a ration to her maids.
She considers a field and buys it; from the fruit of her handiwork
    she plants a vineyard.
She girds her loins with might and strengthens her arms.
She senses that her enterprise is good, so her lamp is not
    extinguished at night.

She puts her hand to the distaff, and her palms support the spindle.
She spreads out her palm to the poor and extends her hands to the destitute.
She fears not snow for her household, for her entire household is clothed with scarlet wool.
Bedspreads she makes herself; linen and purple wool are her clothing.
Well-known at the gates is her husband as he sits with the elders of the land.
Garments she makes and sells, and she delivers a belt to the peddler.
Strength and splendor are her clothing, and smilingly she awaits her last day.
She opens her mouth with Wisdom, and the teaching of kindness is on her tongue.
She anticipates the needs of her household, and the bread of idleness, she does not eat.
Her children rise and celebrate her; and her husband, he praises her:
"Many daughters have attained valor, but you have surpassed them all."
False is grace, and vain is beauty; a God-fearing woman, she should be praised.
Give her the fruit of her hands, and she will be praised at the gates by her very own deeds.

Proverbs 31:10-31

Eshet Chayil

A woman of valor, who can find? Far beyond pearls is her value.

This hymn, taken from the *Book of Proverbs* (31:10-31), is chanted each Friday evening before the Sabbath meal begins.

It is an alphabetical acrostic, with the first letter of each verse representing another letter of the alphabet. Thus, the first word is *Eshet* (beginning with an *Aleph*), the first word of the second verse is *Batach* (beginning with a *Bet*), etc.

To this day the term *Eshet Chayil*, a Woman of Valor, is used by Jews to describe the finest type of Jewish homemaker and helpmate. When we say of a woman that "she was a true *Eshet Chayil*," we mean that she was a devoted wife and mother who observed Jewish law and tradition to the letter. She is the type of woman who deserves the praise that our Sages gave to the matriarchs Sarah and Rebecca (*Bereishit Rabbah* 60:16): "As long as Sarah lived, a cloud hung over her tent. When she died, the cloud departed. When Rebecca came, it returned. As long as Sarah lived, her doors were open wide. When she died, they were closed. When Rebecca came, they were opened again. As long as Sarah lived, there was a blessing on her dough, and the lamp used to burn from the evening of the Sabbath until the evening of the following Sabbath. When she died, these stopped. When Rebecca came they returned."

God Bless You!

The Children of Israel Today

S tanding on the threshold of the twenty-first century, the Children of Israel are finally evolving into that which their ancestors hoped for over three thousand years ago. This evolution necessitates an honest assessment — a soul searching, if you will — by the Jewish people. Once this occurs, Jews and non-Jews will understand more fully who the Jewish people are and what their Torah is.

However, to understand what and who the community of Israel is, one must first comprehend the true meaning of Adam (Man). As stated in Genesis, "Then said God, 'Let us make Man in our image, in our likeness.'" Soon after, however, comes the following verse: "So God created Man in His own image, in the image of God created He him: male and female created He them." These verses suggest a contradiction. Is Adam male or female?

The Book of Proverbs states that the Lord laid the earth's foundations with Wisdom. And throughout the entire Torah, Wisdom is referred to as "She." We can conclude that by gaining Torah wisdom, as our generation must, we will realize the role that both male and female must play in our world.

It must also be obvious that the Jewish people are balancing a very delicate scale to keep the Jewish peoples' growth (as a contributing part of the global community of nations) from annihilating Judaism as a religion.

Soul searching has already caused much disunity, dissension and dissatisfaction among the men and women of Israel: the observant and non-observant; native Israelis and the newly arriving Jews from the Soviet Union, Ethiopia and the four corners of the world. It has also caused resentment toward Jews of the Diaspora who are attempting to rebuild the Jewish homeland from afar by sending financial aid.

For these and many more reasons, Jewish leaders worldwide must take stock of their people and values in a rational, sincere and, above all, wise manner. When all segments of the Jewish community work together for the good of all the Children of Israel, as well as all Mankind, we will have lived up to the task we were chosen for at Sinai when we were appointed guardians of the Ten Commandments.

It was this newly formed nation that was supposed to exemplify what Torah was. And the members of this newly formed family who were most responsible for nurturing and guiding its succeeding generations were the women: the mothers of all the children of the twelve tribes of Israel.

Today, as we stand on the threshold of the twenty-first century, the Jewish Man and especially the Jewish Woman must realize that they are an important link in the great chain that began with Abraham and Sarah, a chain that will end with the coming of *Mashiach*, the Messiah.

Most important of all, however, they must transmit this understanding to their children in an intelligent and sincere fashion. They must ensure the continuity of the chain.

In the past, this continuity was ensured by exposing Jewish children to the teachings of Torah, a living Blueprint of the Universe. This must remain the principal guideline today. But since we are a more mature and sophisticated human race, living daily with science and technology, we must also teach that Right Action and Truth have always been essential to Judaism and the Jewish people, and that to be a True Jew, one must first be a good human being, as illustrated in the account of Noah and the Flood. It would seem logical that to be a True Jew would necessitate being a Good Jew, and thus a good human being. One would have to drop all false illusions about oneself, and the world we live in, to seek out Truth.

The Torah teaches us that only when one searches for Truth, will one reap the fruits of Wisdom and Knowledge. It resulted in a continuity of tradition through unity, pride, heritage and a constant blend of past, present and future, never breaking totally with the past but always building on the chain of history that links past with future.

That chain would have snapped long ago were it not for Israel's deep devotion to Zion, Torah and God, coupled with God's extraordinary relationship with Abraham, Isaac and Jacob, Sarah, Rebecca, Rachel and Leah, Joseph, Yocheved, Miriam, Aaron and Moses. The result: A nation of slaves attained freedom and unity. It became, in fact, one family, with a mission to help free all of humanity, transforming the human race into one family with one God.

Although rarely acknowledged publicly, the family member most responsible for this task was the Jewish Woman: The *Eshet Chayil.*

Throughout the Torah, whenever the Children of Israel were at risk, it was a woman who did what had to be done to foster their faith or prevent their destruction. The stories abound: Sarah kept her anguish silent when she knew that her only son Isaac was to undergo the ultimate test of faith. Rebecca made sure that her husband's legacy was transferred to the wiser of her sons, Jacob, instead of Isaac's favorite son, Esau. Yocheved, Moses' mother, convinced her reluctant husband to father another child, placing her faith in God as she set that child adrift on the Nile. If not for her courage, and that of her daughter Miriam, we would not have been given the Torah through Moses. No one can know for sure whether we would have received it at all.

Less famous, but no less extraordinary women fill the Torah: Tamar, Judah's daughter-in-law, had to impersonate a harlot to ensure the continuity of the tribe that gave us King David - and that will give us (may it be soon!) the Messiah. Rachav, a real harlot, emerged as an *Eshet Chayil* when she hid the spies whom Joshua had sent to investigate Jericho. Risking her life to do so, she enabled the Israelites to conquer Canaan by using her home as a fortress. As legend has it, she went on to accept the God of Israel and became Joshua's wife.

Then there is Ruth the Moabite. Were it not for her Wisdom, Love, Courage and Altruism, King David never would have been born. And Esther sacrificed her girlhood dreams of Jewish domesticity to marry Persia's King Achashverosh, thus saving her people from total annihilation.

In contrast, the Torah also illustrates a woman's capacity to go astray, channeling her strengths in the direction of evil. Its account of Eve in the Garden of Eden clarifies how the future of all humanity depended on the Wisdom, or lack of Wisdom, of a single woman.

Today, as we stand once again at a crucial crossroad, Jewish women (*N'shei Chayil*) have the potential to fulfill the prophecy, "In the end is to be found the beginning." They have what it takes to ensure the survival of Judaism and the State of Israel. Moreover, they can and must work with non-Jewish women to ensure the survival of Humanity in a world that has become unstable, violent, materialistic, hateful, unnatural, divisive, false, corrupt, immoral and susceptible to atomic annihilation at any given moment. In short, they must reconfirm their role of *Eshet Chayil*, helping all other women become Women of Valor as well.

Today's women can take their cue from Miriam, the sister of Moses, who led her sisters across a parted sea into which they were afraid to venture. Just as the women of the Exodus went boldly where no one had gone before, so must today's women venture into uncharted waters, setting a new course for the entire planet.

Who is the Jewish Woman? Where is she coming from? Where is she heading? Before we can answer these questions, we first must understand what being a Jew means.

Most simplistically, a Jew is anyone born to a Jewish mother. This criterion established by the State of Israel, enjoys nearly universal acceptance. The State of Israel uses this yardstick to determine who is a Jew.

A more detailed definition, according to Maimonides, would be:

> A Jew is an individual who believes in One God and the Commandments that God set forth on Mount Sinai. Consequently, a Jew is required to observe 613 commandments, including to remember the Sabbath (*Shabbat*) and keep it holy; to celebrate many holidays and fast days, especially *Pesach, Shavu'ot, Rosh Hashanah, Yom Kippur, Sukkot, Simchat Torah, Chanukah* and *Purim*; to recite the *Shema* twice a day; and to study Torah. Torah study sheds light on life's meaning. Torah study clarifies how human beings are supposed to relate to each other.

Unfortunately, not all Jews who fit the simple definition fit the detailed one as well. Some Jews, or perhaps most, look upon the Torah as a mere book, filled with stories similar to fairy tales. They interpret the stories literally; in doing so, they do themselves and the Torah a great injustice.

What a shame that so many of us don't realize that Biblical studies teach us moral lessons that can make us not simply good Jews but, first and foremost, good human beings. The Torah is a book for all of humanity, not solely for the Jews. This is depicted clearly in the account of the Flood: Noah and his family were saved because they were good and righteous human beings. They were not Jews; they preceded Abraham, the first Jew, by ten generations.

Chapter One relates how "God created Adam in His own image; male and female created He them." Our Sages interpret this shift from singular to plural as follows: Originally, Adam was one soul that was both male and female, instructed by God to be fruitful, multiple and dominate the earth.

Genesis: Chapter Two presents an apparent contradiction: Even though Adam already had been created, "there was not a man to till the soil." God then created a body for Adam out of earth and breathed life into it. When that body was activated, God realized that it had to be separated into its two halves, and so came Eve out of the oneness of Adam. Until the events described in Chapter Two, Adam was just a soul without a body. Male and Female was Adam.

What, you might ask, has all this to do with the Jewish Woman? It clarifies that God created Man male and female, as one soul, in His image. Later, He breathed that combined Soul (named Adam) into one body created for that soul. Realizing that only He could create out of a Oneness, God separated the Human Body into two. Separate but equal, these two aspects of this newly created Body and Soul, called Adam and Eve (*Ish v'Ishah*) worked with, and opposite, each other to create a third being, Seth. And so began the Adamic Race.

Perhaps if we, like God, saw men and women as equal partners, instead of opponents in a power struggle, we would acknowledge that each sex is only half of a very complex species. We would work together eagerly as equal (but not necessarily identical) colleagues. We would respect each gender's innate qualities and both genders' shared intellectual abilities. Perhaps this respect would eliminate the need for equal rights amendments and movements.

I am convinced that women still living in an oppressive environment could dramatically alter it by insisting on equality, but not necessarily equivalence; by channeling the feminine Wisdom at their very fingertips instead of behaving in aggressive, stereotypically masculine ways. With a whisper, not a whine or a shout, women could expose Nature's Truths to those now unable to see them.

At the Jewish woman's disposal is a unique tool to help her reveal these Truths to society. That tool is the Wisdom of Torah, so often depicted as water, a commonality humans cannot live without. However, she must use the Torah's esoteric Wisdom, for that is the frequency feminine Wisdom is tuned into. Permit me to explain:

There is a well-known saying: "One picture is worth a thousand words." A somewhat less known saying corroborates the first: "The most important knowledge is impossible to put into words." One has to get a picture of that knowledge in order to grasp and accept it.

Torah Wisdom must be viewed in this fashion. The Jewish woman is biologically equipped to grasp it more effectively than her male counterpart. She is like a television set, attuned to a transmitting station called Torah. By tuning in properly, she can receive Torah Wisdom concerning her world and her life — as well as life in general. (If only men could be helped to tune in to this Torah frequency via their link to the Tree of Wisdom and Knowledge! Then we would see a new understanding of Torah in our world.)

Since a picture is worth a thousand words, let's use the television as our model for understanding Torah frequency. We know that television waves surround us at all times, but we don't see a picture on our screen unless we turn on our TV set and tune in to the channel we want to watch. The same is true of Torah Wisdom: It surrounds us at all times, but we can't receive the picture, Torah's transmission, unless we tune in properly.

Television or Torah: In both cases it is simply up to us to tune in properly to get the proper picture. With television, we tune in and get entertainment, news, sports and possibly education (and let's not forget advertisements!) being transmitted by the TV stations. With Torah, we tune in and get a picture of what Life is all about. We tune in and learn how to live a simple, natural, spiritual and moral life. We tune in and learn how to regulate ourselves, how to be focused properly at all times.

Because she is constantly open to, and in touch with, the secrets of Nature that Torah conveys, the Jewish woman is more skilled at teaching the Torah way of life. Where does her receptivity come from? Perhaps it comes from her miraculous ability to conceive, to carry life inside her, to bring that life into our world and to raise it into a human being. Perhaps it comes from teaching her children about the laws of nature, and how those laws relate to humankind as well as the animal kingdom. Perhaps it came from being her children's first teacher, acquainting them with time, weather, the seasons and our sources of nourishment, mentioned in the different blessings we recite over food. Most importantly, the Jewish woman acquires her unique receptivity by teaching her children to love and respect Nature and her laws, for they are God's laws; and to love and respect their own feelings (both positive and negative), through which life's hidden mysteries are revealed to us.

Needless to say, the Jewish woman could never accomplish this enormous task without a deep understanding of Torah. That understanding is the reason she was always called an Eshet Chayil.

Certainly, the Jewish man has understood Torah in his own way, interpreting it according to a man's understanding. In this fashion, throughout our history, both men and women created a balanced society within the Jewish community.

Today's generation, however, is dealing with a totally different set of circumstances. The overwhelming majority of America's mainstream Jews has gravitated to suburbia and away from traditional Jewish life. Typically, the husband is harried in the financial world while the wife is caught up in the materialism of suburban or city life, and very often work as well. They both go their separate ways each day while, most of the time, their children are left to take care of themselves.

Some families depend on maids; other depend on drugs. They have abandoned virtually all of their Jewish heritage and have nothing left to fill the void. Spiritually on their own, they must learn to balance the changes they have brought to Judaism with those imposed on them by the non-Jewish world.

Unfortunately, most are unable to do this. In fact, the only person who can achieve that balance is the Jewish woman. But, tragically, she has become like a bird who has left her mother's nest, unable to build her own because she has forgotten her mother's ways. She is floundering in her relatively new-found freedom, lacking a modern role model from whom to learn.

It is imperative for the Jewish woman of this century to accept the great responsibility that is hers: to perpetuate Judaism and the Jewish family as a twenty-first century *Eshet Chayil*; to balance the scale of Torah for both the Jewish and non-Jewish world.

It is up to today's *Eshet Chayil* to begin to understand Torah and to share that understanding with all Humankind. She must begin with the beginning, of course, and come full circle as the twenty-first century Eve, offering Humanity the fruits of both the Tree of Life and the Tree of Wisdom and Knowledge. This *Eshet Chayil* must acquaint all people with the notion that men and women are equal but not the same. She must also educate her sons and daughters to balance the laws of man with the laws of nature, which is the Wisdom of God. And she must help non-Jewish women to do the same, so that the human race will observe the Laws of Noah and understand more clearly what the Torah stands for.

While the Jewish man considers himself one of God's Chosen People, the Jewish woman must redefine the term "Chosen" in a non-elitist fashion. As the first teacher of Good and Evil, she must supersede the moral obligations of man. Why? Not only because she was chosen at Sinai to perpetuate the Ten Commandments but, first and foremost, because she is Nature's caretaker, bearing the human race within her.

That is why the Jewish woman must not do what the Women's Movement would have her do: abandon her responsibility as primary caretaker during her children's formative years.

Of course, many mothers have to work; for them, day care is a necessity. Nevertheless, we must create new ways to care for children of working mothers, ways that will promote flexibility, enabling each mother to spend quality time with her children. We must not delay. The future of humankind is at stake.

When we have met this objective, the twenty-first century *Eshet Chayil* will be able to mold the lives she has conceived and carried. And once she will have completed the molding process, she will be able to stand back and say, "It is good."

Civilization will perish or survive, depending on choices made by the twenty-first century *Eshet Chayil*. But before she can create a better world, she must create a better Jewish society. It all starts with a proper understanding of the word Adam. That understanding will enable men and women to work together to create a better Judaism, a better State of Israel and a better Community of Israel worldwide.

As we stand on the threshold of the twenty-first century, today's Jewish woman must set a good example for the Jewish women of tomorrow. She must help Jewish men understand their role as co-creators of tomorrow's family, tomorrow's Israel and tomorrow's world.

To achieve this, the *Eshet Chayil* must help all Jews realize that their level of observance doesn't make them better or worse Jews. She must convince them that each Jew is judged for his or her actions by God alone (that is why we stand before Him on *Rosh Hashanah* and *Yom Kippur*). If the Children of Israel can't accept and love one another, in spite of their differences, then they have failed as individuals and as a nation.

To circumvent that failure, the Children of Israel can look back to Adam and Eve's journey through time, seeing it with the wisdom we have acquired at this point in our journey. Then they will be able to integrate Torah Wisdom with the technological and scientific advancements civilization has made thus far. By blending old and new — traditional ethics with modern sophistication — we will see the emergence of a truly united and strong Judaism, and State of Israel.

By displaying this role model of unity, peace and harmony to the rest of Humanity, the Community of Israel finally will fulfill the task for which they were chosen at Mount Sinai: to give the light of God and Torah, that is the Blueprint of the Universe, to the rest of the nations of the world.

As in the Beginning,
So in the End

Zohar I; (266) and Epilogue
Part II, Paragraph 4

This is the Jewish Woman's greatest task: to teach her Male counterpart of Adam that a Whole Jew first must be a Whole Human Being. And for the Human Race to be whole, it must be both Male and Female, in proper balance.

If we could merge this understanding with the Inner Knowledge and Wisdom of the Torah and its Laws, as well as with the Oneness of all things — and put this understanding into practice at all times — we would create a Jew that has never been before. This would be a Jew that Abraham, Isaac, Jacob, Joseph and Moses dreamed of; a Jew that Sarah, Rebecca, Rachel, Leah, Yocheved and Miriam imagined; a Jew that King David and King Solomon wrote of; a Jew that will show Humanity how to live and contribute to Life in the best way, how to make this world a better place for our children and all the children of future generations.

The Female aspect of Adam must play this vital role; this is what she was created for. And she can do it, if she would only set her mind to it, for she is the physical representative of the Shechinah (the Divine Presence), with all the Wisdom which that implies.

She can begin her mission as the twenty-first century *Eshet Chayil* by helping all women to assume their rightful role within the history of Humankind, to create a true Sisterhood/Brotherhood of Humanity and to grow as a Tree of Life.

Worldwide, the women of the Community of Israel must begin by finding a unifying factor in their history to which they can all relate. That factor is the Light of *Shabbat* which they usher in each week by lighting the *Shabbat* candles.

The second unifying factor that Jewish women must perpetuate is *Kashrut* (Jewish dietary laws). Some women will observe *Kashrut* strictly, others liberally, still others not at all. But in all cases, *Kashrut* will be bequeathed to succeeding generations as a unifying principle.

And the third factor is one that even the Israeli Government adheres to: *Taharat Hamishpacha* (Laws of Family Purity). If the groom's family does not place a two-week ad in the Israeli newspapers (to assure the groom's eligibility), and if the bride does not immerse herself in a mikva (ritualarium), the government does not consider the wedding legitimate.

The Israeli government defines a Jew as anyone born to a mother who is Jewish by birth or by conversion by an Orthodox rabbi according to *halachah* (Jewish law). It is possible that the leaders of that government do not realize where this law stems from and why it is so necessary. If all Jewish women knew that the continuity of a species's purity is solely up to those who bear its young, perhaps all Jews would accept the laws of *Taharat Hamishpacha*.

We do not wish to suggest that one segment of Humanity is pure or better than the rest. We do not wish to infer that all of Humanity must subscribe to one religion, or perhaps relinquish religion altogether, once the Human Race becomes a Brotherhood. We do wish to assert that many different species of Life were created to give us all the necessary elements required to make this world function harmoniously, just as many instruments are needed to create beautiful, harmonious music, just as many colors are needed to create a beautiful painting.

If the Jewish women everywhere would unite, they could create a network based on the three principles that comprise a triangle of faith and responsibility. They could then help their male counterparts of Adam to unite and to commit to the male triangle of responsibility:

1) To be fruitful and multiply, and not to spill their seed (a very important link to Family Purity and the *B'chorah*);

2) To till the soil and create a more abundant world for all (a vital element in the Laws of *Kashrut*);

3) To be strong through Wisdom from the transfer of *Shabbat*'s energy through the tradition of having marital relations on Friday night.

Only then will we witness *ISH V'ISHA*, Male and Female, the two sides of Adam working together as they were meant to in the Garden of Eden. Together, the Children of Israel will finally become the Living Shield, the Star of David.

Perhaps, when this can be achieved, we will understand why King Solomon wrote: "*Eshet Chayil mi yimtza, v'rachok mipninim mikrah...Pi'ha patchah b'chochmah, v'Torat chesed al l'shonah.*"

"A Woman of Valor, who can find? Far beyond pearls is her value... She opens her mouth with wisdom, and the teaching of kindness is on her tongue."

Let us hope that this is just The Beginning.

Jeremiah

Jeremiah said: "When I was going back to Jerusalem I lifted up my eyes and saw a woman sitting at the top of the mountain. She was clothed in black, her hair disheveled, crying and pleading for someone to comfort her. I, too, was crying and pleading "Who will comfort me?" I approached her and spoke to her, saying: "If you are a woman, speak to me, but if you are a spirit, depart from me."

She answered: "I am your Mother, Zion." I told her: "God will comfort you ... Flesh and blood built you, flesh and blood destroyed you. But in the time-to-come, says the Lord, I will rebuild you."

Thus it is written in Psalm 147:2, "*Bonei Yerushalayim Hashem* (God is the Builder of Jerusalem), *nidchei Yisrael y'kaness* (He will gather together the dispersed of Israel)." *Amen.* Soon and in our own days, may the Holy One, blessed be He, fulfill the prophecy that says of us (Isaiah 35:10): "*Uf duyei Hashem yishuvun uva'u Tzion b'rinah v'simchat olam al rosham; sasson v'simchah yasigu, v'nasu yagon va'anachah*" (And the ransomed of Hashem shall return to Zion with songs and everlasting joy upon their heads; they shall obtain joy and gladness; sorrow and sighing shall flee away).

The Shechinah

Throughout the Torah and Talmud, the Shechinah (meaning God's Beloved, according to the Zohar) is referred to in many ways: Torah, Wisdom, the Community of Israel, the Holy Presence, the Rose of Sharon, the Rose of the Valley, the Lilly of the Valley, Hashulamit, Zion, Binah, G'vurah, Hod and Malchut, to name a few.

However, the Zohar's reference to the word Shechinah deserves special mention. The Zohar states that the first Heh in the Tetragrammaton (YHVH, God's name) stands for Binah (the Mother); the second Heh stands for Malchut (the Kingdom of Earth that we live in); top point of the Yod stands for Keter (the Kingdom of Heaven, the Crown); the Yod itself stands for Chochmah (the Father); and the Vav symbolizes, among other things, the grades of the six days of Creation.

The Zohar does not hesitate to declare that the Whole of the Torah is the Holy Name — YHVH.

This being the case, we can understand why both Male and Female, Husband and Wife, Father and Mother, will both be needed for Mashiach to be with us. For we read in the Zohar (V'etchanan 260b), "Thou hast begun to show thy Servant." Why is a beginning mentioned here? Because Moses indeed made a new beginning in the world by being complete in all. It is true that Jacob was also complete and in him the tree was completed below after the pattern above. Yet there was in Moses that which was not in any other man, since his perfection radiated to many thousands and myriads of Israelites in the Tabernacle: the priests, the Levites, the twelve tribes with their chieftains, the seventy members of the *Sanhedrin* — in fact, with the perfect body, Aaron being at the right, Nachshon at the left, he himself in the center, as it says here "thy greatness," referring to Aaron, and "thy strong hand," referring to Nachshon. Thus Moses was a new beginning in the world.

And if you ask, "Who is the termination?" the answer is: The King Messiah. For when he arrives (may it be soon!), there shall be a perfection in the world that has not been for all generations before. For then, and only then, there shall be completeness above and below.

> ON THAT DAY, THE LORD SHALL BE ONE AND HIS
>   NAME ONE.
> BAYOM HAHU, YIHIYEH ADONAI ECHAD USH'MO
>   ECHAD.

Zechariah, 14:9

> In that day there will be a highway from Egypt to Assyria.
> The Egyptians and Assyrians will worship together.
> In that day Israel will be the third, along with Egypt and
> Assyria, a blessing on the earth.
> The Lord Almighty will bless them, saying, "Blessed be
> Egypt — my people, Assyria — my handiwork, and Israel — my
> inheritance."

Isaiah 19:23-25[43]

> ANI L'DODI V'DODI LI
> I am my beloved and my beloved is me.

Song of Songs
or
Solomon's Songs 3:16

FOOTNOTES

1. See *Zohar* 1:118a: "As the Messianic Era approaches, even 'children' will be able to understand the most hidden secrets of the *Kabbalah*..." This passage is cited by Rabbi Chaim Vital in his introduction to *Sha'ar Hahakdamot* (Attieh edition), p. 3b-c, reproduced at the beginning of *Etz Chaim* (Attieh edition), p. 6 (3d). Rabbi Chaim then adds: "In the final generation, this wisdom will become revealed and publicized. People will then be able to understand inner secrets of the Torah that previous generations were not able to grasp fully. This invalidates the question, 'If previous generations were unable to understand, how can we?'"

    The final generation's ability to understand more deeply is not because it will be on a higher level than its predecessors. Rather, the revelation of these secrets that began with the *Zohar*, the Ari, etc. is reaching its climax. Even *ruach hakodesh* (Divine inspiration) will be available in the final generation, albeit in hidden and obscure ways. This is because the process of revelation and *ruach hakodesh* is filtering down slowly, clothed in many phenomena of the times. For a proof of this, see ibid., p. 8, quoting the *Tikunei Zohar Chadash* (Mossad Rav Kook), p. 103a: "You, Eliahu, will precede all the prophets in the generation preceding the coming of the Messiah. There are those to whom you will reveal yourself hiddenly [covertly], through the intellect of the mind. There are those to whom you will reveal yourself through [received] wisdom, and there are those to whom you will manifest yourself in a physical body, face to face" (Rabbi Chaim Vital, ibid.).

The statement, "hiddenly [covertly], through the intellect of the mind," also includes an understanding of the natural wisdom inherent in creation through the teachings of the *Kabbalah*, and vice versa. This is discussed at length in the book, *Kol Hator*, by Rabbi Hillel Rivlin of Shklov, in the name of his teacher, the Gaon of Vilna; see footnote 4 in Epilogue.

The Zohar's statement that the revelation of the secrets of *Kabbalah* will take place in the generation of the Messiah means before, not after, his arrival. It is for this reason that the *Zohar* speaks of the "generation" of the coming of Messiah, not the coming of Messiah himself (Rabbi Isaac DeLattesh, letter of approbation, printed before*Zohar Bereishit*). This is what is meant by "we have evolved and matured enough," etc.

2. See *Yevamot* 63a, where Rabbi Eliezer says, "Any man who does not have a wife is not Adam, as it is written, `Male and female He created them, and He called their name Adam'" (Genesis 5:2). The Yismach Yisrael elucidates: If a person does not give of him or herself to another, then he or she is defeating the purpose of creation and the underlying principle of Adam." (See next note.) See also *Zohar* 1:47a: "`Let us make Adam' — This is the secret of male/female." See *Zohar* 2:144b: "Everything that God made from top to bottom is all in the secret of male/female... The term Adam always refers to male/female." See *Baba Batra* 74b: "Everything that the Holy One, Blessed be He, created in His world is male/female." See *Zohar* 1:157b: "Rabbi Yossi said, `There is nothing in the universe that is not male/female.'" See *Zohar*

3:7b: "Rabbi Shimon said, `The union of male and female is called "one" because a male without the female is only half a body. Half or part is not one.'"

See *Sefer Yetzirah* 3:1, GRA ad. loc. s.v. *Zachar U'nekeva* ("Male/Female"). See *Zohar* 3:81b, 3:109b, 3:143b, 3:296a. See *Etz Chaim* 10:3, 38:2; *Sha'ar Hap'sukim* (Ashlag edition, Jerusalem), p. 17; *Likutei Torah* (Ashlag), pp. 29, 31. All these sources together yield the following fascinating information:

The numerical value of Adam is 45: *Aleph* = 1, *Dalet* = 4, *Mem* = 40, which is equal to the Divine Name, YHVH, when each letter,*Yod-Keh-Vav-Keh*, is spelled out in full:*Yod-Vav-Dalet* = 20, *Heh-Aleph* = 6, *Vav-Aleph*-Vav = 13, *Heh-Aleph* = 6.

When the initial letters of the Divine Name are taken alone, they equal 26: *Yod* = 10, *Heh*= 5, Vav = 6, *Heh* = 5. When these initial letters are omitted from the fully spelled out name, whose numerical value is 45, the remaining letters (*Vav-Dalet* = 10, *Aleph* = 1, *Aleph-Vav* = 7, *Aleph* = 1) yield a total of 19, the numerical value of Eve (*Chava*): *Chet* = 8, *Vav* = 6, *Heh* = 5.

The same symmetry is obtained when the Divine Name of 45 is split down the middle. The first two letters spelled out (Yod-Vav-Dalet = 20, *Heh-Aleph* = 6) yield 26! The second two letters spelled out (*Vav-Aleph-Vav* = 13, *Heh-Aleph* = 6) yield 19!

Thus, in two highly significant ways, the Divine Name of 45 is a special combination of 26 plus 19 = 45 = Adam. The first method of extracting the initial letters for the male (26), with the remaining letters being left for the female (19), is the parallel [or inner counterpart] of the tradition that Eve was extracted from Adam's side or rib. This means that 45 = Adam is the male aspect of *Yod-Keh-Vav-Keh* = 26, while the Female, inner aspect of the Name equals Chava = 19.

The second method of splitting the Divine Name down the middle is the parallel [or inner counterpart] of the tradition that Adam and Eve were themselves back to back and split down the middle!

```
10  ë
 5  ä
 6  à
 5  ä
───
26
```

```
 1  ç              8  ç
 4  â
                   6  à
40  ì              5  ä
───               ───
45                19
```

One way which yields 45 is:

```
10  ââ     +    ë  10   =   ââë 20
 1  ç      +    ä   5   =   çä   6
 7  àç     +    à   6   =   àçà 13
 1  ç      +    ä   5   =   çä   6
───             ───         ───
19         +       26   =       45
```

The second way which yields 45 is:

ââë20 + çä6 = 26

àçà13 + çä6 = 19

```
          ───
           45
```

3. See previous note. See *Zohar* 2:176b: "Until there was a balance (matkala, literally, `scale') they were not able to consummate `face to face.'" This is one of the pivotal points in *Kabbalah* and in this book. The *Zohar* calls the balance of any state, matkala, the scale that balances all of its opposing parts together into a gestalt, known as a *Partzuf* in the teachings of Rabbi Isaac Luria (the Ari). The "parts" that express this gestalt are called *Sefirot*. When all the *Sefirot* relate as a whole, together, they are called a *Partzuf*. By definition, therefore, a *Partzuf* is "a whole that is greater that the sum of its parts."

The concept of *Partzuf* is intimately related to that of *Tikun*, "rectification" or "mending." (The Hebrew word *Tikun* is related to the Latin techne, as in technology.) It is only in the "Universe of *Tikun*" that a *Partzuf* comes into being, precisely because it represents the ability of many diverse forces to function together in a harmonious fashion. This is obviously the secret of all *Tikun*.

The opposite of *Tikun* is *Tohu*, chaos. In the "Universe of Tohu" that preceded that of *Tikun*, there was no balance, only opposites opposing and cancelling each other out (in Hebrew, it is called tohu, which is also related to the word tao). See *The Bahir*, Wieser (1979), translated by Rabbi Aryeh Kaplan, pp. 1, 88-90. Our job then is to mend and reconcile these opposites in ourselves, in all of humanity, and in the spiritual/physical universe. This creates a unification and balance of forces (*Partzuf*) to come into existence, which is capable of channeling the powerful revelation of God's light in a reciprocal union with the whole universe. This is brought about by the Jewish people through their keeping the Torah's commandments, and by non-Jews through their keeping the Seven Noahide laws. This is the balance and unification of Adam. See the GRA on Sifra DeTzeniuta, pp. 1-2. This is also known in philosophy as thesis-antithesis-synthesis. The synthesis is the balance of the former two

(*Sefer Yetzirah*, Chapter 2, translated by Rabbi Aryeh Kaplan, Wieser (1991), p. 95). See *Leshem Sh'vo V'achlamah, Sefer D'rushei Olam Hatohu (De'ah)* 1:2:4, p. 12 (6d).

4. This is explained later on.

5. See Jerusalem Talmud, *Shabbat* 11b: Adam was the flame of the world, and since Eve put out Adam's flame (caused him to die), she was given the commandment to light the Sabbath candles, bringing Adam's light back into the universe.

6. See footnote 1. With our limited understanding, it looks like the old is discarded. In terms of the greater picture, however, when the new is introduced, both old and new are incorporated into a single gestalt. Their distinctiveness is thus preserved, producing a "greater whole that is greater than the sum of the parts." See *Etz Chaim* (Attieh edition), Volume 2, p. 237 (119a), s.v. *L'Ha'Ari*: "Previous generations spoke of ten *Sefirot* (`parts') without explicitly relating them to *Partzufim* (`wholes'), because the illumination of these emanations hadn't unfolded yet... Nowadays, however, these illuminations have began to unfold..." i.e., we now have the ability to see the *Sefirot* (parts and entities) in terms of their larger contexts, the *Partzufim* (in gestalted structures). See Rabbi Chaim David Yosef Azulai (the*Chida*),*Shem Hag'dolim, Aleph*, no. 219 (small print), p. 21 (11a). Based on the above statement, the *Chida* explains that the Ari apparently taught certain things that were not mentioned in previous texts. He also explains why the *Zohar*, the ancient Kabbalistic text attributed to Rabbi Shimon bar Yochai, was not revealed until the 13th century (beginning of the 6th millennium): "because the time for its revelation had not yet arrived." For a deeper understanding of this, see Rabbi Shlomo Eliyashiv, *Leshem Sh'vo V'achlamah, Sefer Biurim*, p. 21b s.v. *Klallo Shel Davar*, and 21d s.v. *V'hinei*: "What was forbidden to investigate and expound upon just yesterday becomes permissible today. This is felt by every true exegete. Many matters whose awesome nature repelled one from even approaching in

previous generations are easily grasped today. This is because the gates of human understanding below have been opened up as a result of *the steadily increasing flow of Divine revelations above.*" This will explain one of this book's most important themes.

7. Wilson, Ian. *Exodus: The True Story Behind The Biblical Account.* New York: Harper & Row, 1985.

8. Johnson, Ken. *The Ancient Magic of the Pyramids.* New York: Simon & Schuster, 1977.

9. Ibid.

10. Nightingale, Florence. *Letters From Egypt, A Journey on the Nile.* London: Weidenfeld & Nicolson reprinting of Barrie & Jenkins, Ltd., 1887.

11. Newman, Louis I. *The Hasidic Anthology.* New York: Schocken Books, 1963.

12. Ibid.

13. Ibid.

14. Kaplan, Aryeh. *The Handbook of Jewish Thought.* New York: Moznaim, 1979. *Zohar* 2:34a; *Leshem Sh'vo V'achlamah, Sefer D'rushei Olam Hatohu (De'ah),* 2:4:20:3, p. 164 (82c): "It is written in the Torah, `Come to Pharaoh,' not `Go to Pharaoh.' Why is this? To teach you that God brought Moses into the inner chambers of the Great Serpent (of Egypt), the root of all Egyptian wisdom." See *Zohar* 1:76a: "He gave wisdom to Moses. This is the meaning of the verse, `My servant Moses is [like] a trusted servant throughout My entire house' (Numbers 12:7). There has never been anyone like Moses who was able to enter all levels [of defilement] when he descended into the depths of Egyptian wisdom that comes from the `Other Side' of the Primordial Serpent. For his heart remained steadfast in the face of all their entice-ments. He remained trustworthy to the great supernal faith." In other words, Moses was able to perceive God's Unity in

everything. Nothing, including the powerful occult forces of ancient Egypt, exists independently of God. See *Sanhedrin* 67a; Ramchal, *Da'at Tevunot* (Bnei Brak, 1975), pp. 12-13.

15. See *Mechiltah* Exodus 12:38.

16. Leviticus 23:5.

17. Ibid., 23:3.

18. Ibid., 23:9-19.

19. Ibid., 23:33-42.

20. Ibid., 25:1-23.

21. Dobin, Joel C. *The Astrological Secrets of the Hebrew Sages.* New York: Inner Traditions, Ltd., 1983.

22. See *Derech Hashem* (The Way of God) by Rabbi Moshe Chaim Luzzato, Feldheim, 1983, 4:7:6 pg. 319.

23. See Ramban, Genesis 25:33. Ibid., Rabbeinu B'chaya :31; *Sha'ar Hap'sukim* of the Ari, p. 10c, loc. *v'hinei; Sha'ar Hamitzvot* on honoring parents, p. 14b-15. *Sha'ar Hakavanot* p. 23a, loc. v'hinei; *Etz Chaim* 39:8. "The parents give from their physical components to the physical and spiritual aspects of their children. This is in order to be a vehicle to 'carry' and elicit their children's soul ... The *oldest* son takes the main share of this 'allotment,' and the other brothers and sisters take their share from that which remains from the 'physical and spiritual components' that come through the oldest son. Through this, we can understand to some extent the commandment of honoring our parents." See Rabbeinu B'chaya, *Kad Hakemach*, on honoring parents; Maharal of Prague, *G'vurot Hashem*: 29.

24. See Ramban, Genesis 2:7; *Zohar* 1:27a; Deuteronomy 32:9 in conjunction with Job 31:2. See *Or Hachaim*, Deuteronomy 32:8, second half. *Shiur Komah* of Rabbi Moshe Cordevero, p. 55 loc. Vayifach: "One who blows out a breath is blowing from his innermost insides." *Emek Hamelech, Sha'ar Olam*

Hatohu: 31 end (p. 20) Ibid p. 121d. "The [highest aspect of] soul comes from His (God's) essence." *Shefa Tal* of Rabbi Shabtai Horowitz of Prague, p. 46, note. This is said in particular of the highest aspect of the soul, see *Etz Chaim* 42:1.

25. Five levels of soul, see *Bereishit Rabbah* 14:9; Ari, *Sha'ar Hagilgulim:* 1; Ramchal (Rabbi Moshe Chaim Luzzatto), *Derech Hashem* (The Way of God) 3:1:4. The first level of soul from the bottom up is divided into two parts: the lower part or phase is the animal soul, and its highest phase is the "higher soul of man" called *nefesh.* Ramchal, ibid. *Tanya* 1:1-2. Concerning their connection from one soul to the other, see *Nefesh Hachaim* of Rabbi Chaim Volozhin 1:14-19. Since the highest level of soul is called the "portion from God above," so to speak (see footnote 11), it is the highest level of soul representing the ancestral bloodline which is the *B'chorah,* the firstborn.

26. This will happen by acquiring the highest level of soul (*Yechidah*). See Ari, *Likutei Torah, Ki Tisa,* p. 169a (square print) loc. avel. *Likutei Shas* of the Ari, Tractate *Kiddushin.* Since the Messiah is also the royalty of the firstborn, as stated in the *Midrash,* it is understood that this highest aspect of soul is connected to the royalty of the firstborn.

27. See *Targum Yehonatan,* Genesis 3:21; *Tikunei Zohar. Tikun* 58, p. 92b (Mossad HaRav Kook): "that their bodies became identified with the 'skin' of the Serpent." See *Nefesh Hachaim,* 1:6, note, old edition p. 6, new edition, p. 17, loc. "This was before the sin." In other words, before Adam and Eve engaged in the Tree of Knowledge, the enticement to eat from it was not in their psyche, but rather outside of themselves in the form of a snake. Now the Serpent's enticement is identified inside of us through and through. We call it our ego (the evil inclination or *Yetzer Hara*). See *Tanya, Likutei Amorim.* Chapter 22.

28. The reason why the royalty of the firstborn was exiled into Egypt is clear from our text here. See Epilogue, Part II. For the basic ideas concerning the Serpent turning into a staff and usurping Egypt's power, exemplified by the firstborn, see *Kinot Hashem Tzva'ot* by Rabbi Moshe Chaim Luzzatto, B'nei Brak, Friedlander, p. 98-99. Lectures of Rabbi Shimom Kessin, New York. *Zohar* 2:34. All this explains why Pharaoh killed only the males, that is, to stop the continuation of the ancestral bloodline. This is why Jews were given the commandment to redeem each male firstborn and to sanctify the male firstborn of domestic animals by bringing them to the Temple Altar.

29. The basic ideas on the synchronization of time between the sun and the moon are taken from Rabbi Meir ibn Gabbai, *Avodat Hakodesh, Chelek Sitrei Torah* 2 (Lewin-Epstein, 1954), pp. 228-229; Rabbi Shlomo Eliyashiv, *Leshem Sh'vo V'achlamah, De'ah* 2:4:9, pp. 209-210 (105b-c). See also *Pirkei Rabbi Eliezer* 8, Radak no. 8.

30. See Jerusalem Talmud, Ketubot 1:2 p. 5b, ibid. *Nedarim* 6:8 p. 16b.

31. See *Leshem Sh'vo V'achlamah, De'ah* 1:6:4:5, p. 150 (75c-d). Even though we speak of synchronized time every 19 years, mathematically a difference remains of one hour and 26.9 minutes. This will only be rectified in the Ultimate Future.

32. The basic ideas about the Torah, the First and Second Tablets, etc., are drawn from *Zohar* 1:26b. *Tikunei Zohar* 40 (80b), *Sha'ar Ma'amarei Chazal* (Attieh edition), p. 16a, on *Avot*, s.v. Rebbi Meir, (Ashlag edition), p. 80a. See GRA, *Even Shleimah*, Chapter 11, p. 104; Rabbi Eliahu Dessler, *Michtav Me'Eliahu*, Volume 2, pp. 27, 29-30. Ramchal, *Da'at Tevunot* (Bnei Brak, 1975), pp. 112-114. On the purification of the physical, see ibid, pp. 53-62, 73-84. On the inner light, see *Yalkut Shimoni*, Yeshayahu 60, section 499; *Leshem Sh'vo V'achlamah, Hakdamot U'She'arim*, p. 63. On the study of

Kabbalah before the arrival of the Messiah, see footnote 5: *Zohar, Raya Mahemna* 3:124b; Rabbi Chaim Vital, Introduction to *Etz Chaim*. See also the GRA, *Even Shleimah* 11:3.

33. This is usually expressed in Torah sources as the idea of the Shmittah (a cycle of Seven, hence Sabbatical). Thus, there are seven cycles of 7,000 years, each one of an entirely different nature. According to these sources, these seven cycles (49,000 years) is all there is. What comes before or after is not known, or just isn't. However, Rabbi Isaac Luria (the Ari) disputes these opinions. He states:

The entire concept of the *Shmittah* (cycles of seven) is misunderstood. The idea is not, as they say, that there was a universe before this one, and we are now in the second, and therefore, another five cycles must elapse in order to complete the seven cycles. No, this is not the case at all. In truth, the idea of the *Shmittah* (Seven) refers to the seven *Sefirot* of the "Universe of Chaos." These *Sefirot* shattered and were then rectified. It is from these broken *Sefirot* that our present universe, which will last 7,000 years, was brought into existence. This is the sum of the matter (*Sha'ar Ma'amarei Rashbi*) (Attieh edition), p. 44c.

It is important to understand what the Ari intended by this statement. He did not intend to refute the idea of cycles per se. Rather, he wished to correct the mistaken impression that it is all a matter of seven cycles and no more. In truth, it is an ongoing process, wherein each cycle of six or seven thousand years represents one complete *Partzuf* (gestalted whole) that emanates from God's infinite light. The "birth" of each new *Partzuf* is considered the beginning of a new universe or universal cycle. When this *Partzuf* reaches its Sabbath (seventh millennium), it is said to have attained full maturity. However, this maturity is relative, for the process does not end there. Rather, the moment another *Partzuf* emanates from God's infinite light, the previous world or cycle of 6,000 years is lifted up to the level above it. (This previous level itself had once occupied a lower position. Now, with its successor taking its place, it is catapulted to the superposition immediately above. This process goes on ad infinitum.) As we shall now see, this process is described by three key terms: *Tikun* (Rectification), *Birrur* (Purification) and *Aliyah* (Elevation). All this is apparent in the Ari's system of *Kabbalah* and expressed explicitly throughout the writings of Rabbi Shalom Sharabi (the Rashash). The Rashash states:

With the completion of each succeeding cycle of 6,000 years, the entire creation is brought one step higher in its (never ending) process of *Tikun* (Rectification), *Birrur* (Purification) and *Aliyah* (Elevation). This occurs in such a way that each particular level is elevated to the position of the one above it. The reason for this is because a period of 6,000 years is the time allotted for the rectification, purification and elevation of a single universal cycle. Every universal cycle or *Partzuf* (of 6,000 years) is thus regarded as a single step forward and upward at every corresponding level. *Nahar Shalom* (Attieh edition, back of *Etz Chaim*), p. 13b.

Note that the emanation of each new *Partzuf* involves the creation of an entirely new time-space continuum. Prior to the emanation of the *Partzuf*, its space and time do not exist. With all this in mind, we can now understand a deep esoteric passage of the Ari:

Why was the universe created at the particular time it was created and not earlier or later? The universe was created at its particular time because of the process of devolution that had to take place as each successive *Partzuf* and level were emanated from the *Partzuf* and level above. This process, which moves from level to level and from *Partzuf* to *Partzuf*, is what determines the particular time and space for each new cycle. Accordingly, it would not have been possible for our universe to have been created earlier or later. It had to be created in its exact time and space in the (total) order of devolution of levels and *Partzufim*. *Etz Chaim, Sha'ar Igulim V'Yosher* 1 s.v. *Hachakirah Bet* (Attieh edition), p. 21 (11a).

34. The idea of a "unified theory of knowledge" and "as above, so below" are actually the cornerstones of *Kabbalah*. "Below" is a copy of "Above." Despite the multiplicity of phenomena in the universe, with each entity having its own unique character, everything together forms a greater whole. This is discussed in different places in the writings of the great Kabbalist, Rabbi Moshe Chaim Luzzato (the Ramchal). The main idea is that since all things emanate from God's Oneness, they must all reflect that Oneness. This is expressed later in this book as the purpose of perennial philosophy through *Kabbalah*.

35. As explained in the teachings of the Ari, this depends on our own level of purification, together with that of the universe as a whole. For an example of how our perception changes reality, see Rabbi Shlomo Eliyasiv, *Leshem Sh'vo V'achlamah*, *De'ah* 2:4:22:1, p. 176 (88c). He explains the prohibition of staring at a rainbow thus: This staring causes the "unification" of the rainbow in its distorted state, while it is still enclosed in its shell, producing an emanation in a unperfected (solidified) state.

36. It is proper here to quote from *Derech Hatechiyah* (The Road to Renewal), an essay by Rabbi Abraham Isaac Kook:

The aspiration for self-revitalization, for an illumination of the soul as in earlier days, was felt at times in the nation. Sometimes, illuminated spirits of great stature arose, seeking through their psychic powers to stimulate a spiritual renewal among their people and to influence them to recognize that study must be strengthened by the spiritual reality that discloses itself in the course of its unfolding. But the times did not prove opportune for this.

Christianity arose in such an epoch of weakness, and it wrought injury to the nation. Its founder was endowed with a remarkably charismatic personality, and he exerted great spiritual influence, but he had not escaped the defect of idolatry, which is an intensification of spiritual influence without the prior training in the existing moral and cultural disciplines. And he and his followers were so committed to the cultivation of the spiritual life that they lost their Jewish characteristics and became alienated, in deed and spirit, from the source whence they had sprung.

An earlier document concerning the true message of Christianity was a letter to the *Va'ad Arba Aratzot* (Council of the Four Lands), written in 1757 by Rabbi Jacob Emden. Rabbi Harvey Falk, the letter's translator, sheds important light on this historical manuscript:

Rabbi Jacob Emden (1697-1776) was one of the leading Torah authorities of the past several centuries... In his time, he was a fearless champion of Orthodox Judaism. His scholarly stature and endless quest for truth were surely the catalysts responsible for catapulting him into the forefront of the battle against the Shabbatean messianic movement. [Shabbetai Zvi, a 17th century mystic (d. 1676), presented himself as the Messiah, and many Jews initially believed his claim. When the Turks threatened him with death unless he converted to Islam, he meekly acquiesced, expiring in ignominy. However, secret cells of believers still followed his teachings and hoped for new leadership.]...

In Rabbi Emden's time, a group of Polish Shabbateans under the leadership of Jacob Frank posed an enormous threat to the Jewish community of Poland. This group — distorting various Kabbalistic formulas — violated Jewish law and practiced sexual immorality. When excommunicated by the Polish rabbinate, they complained to several Catholic bishops that they were being persecuted by their fellow Jews because they believed in the Trinity. This eventually led to the burning of the Talmud in Poland. The Frankists also sought to revive the notorious blood libel against the Jews.

During this controversy, the Council of the Four Lands — the central institution of Jewish self-government in Poland — turned to Rabbi Emden for guidance. The basic question was whether it was permitted to inform the Polish authorities — both governmental and ecclesiastical — about the true nature of the Frankists. Rabbi Emden not only replied that it was their obligation to do so, no matter what the consequences, but he also advised them to appeal to the Christian community [to support their] struggle against the immoral Frankists and generally to aid the Jews in their observance of the Torah. This led Emden into a thorough analysis of the beginnings of Christianity and especially the original intentions of Jesus and Paul. He believed that the Nazarene and the Apostle to the Gentiles acted entirely within the halachah (Jewish law) in creating a religion for the Gentiles based on the Noahide Commandments, and he interpreted various passages in the Gospels to show that both considered Jewish Law eternally binding upon Jews. [The seven Noahide Commandments consist of the prohibitions against idolatry, blasphemy, killing, stealing, sexual sins, eating the limb of a living animal (cruelty to animals) and the imperative to establish courts of justice. According to the Talmud and Tosefta, those Gentiles who observe these statutes are considered to be of the Chasidim (pious ones) of the Nations and to merit a share in the World to Come.]

Although many Jewish authorities have written positively concerning Christianity, it is clear that Emden went much further. He wrote that Jesus "brought about a double kindness to the world" and that "Paul was a scholar, an attendant of Rabban Gamliel the Elder."

It might be argued that Rabbi Emden wrote this letter at a time of great turmoil and that he may have abandoned his position at a later date. It would be erroneous to assume so,

111

as he frequently reiterated his positive views concerning Christianity — and Islam as well — in his other books. Commenting on the passage, "May all inhabitants of the earth recognize and know..." in the *Aleinu* prayer, Emden wrote: "The proper reason for these words is to pray for the Gentiles; we witness here the greatness of our Sages and their magnanimous desire for [the Gentiles'] true success."

His letter to the Council of the Four Lands appeared as an appendix to his *Seder Olam* (1757) and was republished in his *Sefer Shimmush* (1758-63). The early and final sections of the letter, which deal with the Shabbateans and the internal situation in Poland, are omitted from the translation. The passages on Christianity are given in full.

Rabbi Jacob Emden's letter to the Council of the Four Lands follows:

For it is recognized that also the Nazarene and his disciples, especially Paul, warned concerning the Torah of the Israelites, to which all the circumcised are tied. And if they are truly Christian, they will observe their faith with truth, and not allow within their boundary this new unfit Messiah Shabbetai Zvi who came to destroy the earth.

But truly, even according to the writers of the Gospels, a Jew is not permitted to leave his Torah, for Paul wrote in his letter to the Galatians (Gal. 5) "I, Paul, say to you that if you receive circumcision, the Messiah will do you no good at all. You can take it from me that every man who received circumcision is under obligation to keep the entire Torah." Again, because of this, he admonished in a letter to the Corinthians (1 Cor. 7) that the circumcised should not remove the marks of circumcision, nor should the uncircumcised circumcise themselves.

Many have claimed that Paul appears to contradict himself here. In the Acts of the Apostles (Acts 16), it is mentioned that Paul circumcised his disciple Timothy. They found this very puzzling, for this seems to contradict the latter text which seems to indicate that he considered circumcision a temporary commandment until the Messiah's arrival; but this took place after the time of the Nazarene! Therefore you must realize — and accept the truth from him who speaks it — that we see clearly here that the Nazarene and his Apostles did not wish to destroy the Torah for Israel, God forbid; for it is written so in Matthew (Mt. 5), the Nazarene having said, "Do not suppose that I have come to abolish the Torah. I did not come to abolish, but fulfill. I tell you this: So long as heaven and earth endure, not a letter, not a stroke, will disappear from the Torah until it is achieved. If any man therefore sets aside even the least of the Torah's commandments, and teaches others to do the same, he will have the lowest place in the Kingdom of Heaven, whereas anyone who keeps the Torah, and teaches others to do so, will stand high in the Kingdom of Heaven." This is also recorded in Luke (Lk. 16). It is therefore exceedingly clear that the Nazarene never dreamed of destroying the Torah.

We similarly find Paul, his disciple, in a letter to the Corinthians (1 Cor. 5), accusing them of fornication, and condemning one who lived with his father's wife. You may therefore understand that Paul doesn't contradict himself because of his circumcision of Timothy, for the latter was the son of a Jewish mother and a Gentile father (Acts 16), and Paul was a scholar, an attendant of Rabban Gamliel the Elder, well-versed in the laws of the Torah. He knew that the child of a Jewish mother is considered a full Jew, even if the father should be a Gentile, as is written in the Talmud and Codes. He therefore acted entirely in accordance with the halachah by circumcising Timothy. This would be in line with his position that all should remain within their own faith (1 Cor. 7). Timothy, born of a Jewish mother, had the law of a Jew, and had to be circumcised, just as he was enjoined to observe all commandments of the Torah (Paul's condemnation of the man who lived with his stepmother is similarly understandable, as such an act is also forbidden to Noahides), for all who are circumcised are bound by all the commandments. This provides a satisfactory reply to the question.

This will also solve the apparent contradictions in the Nazarene's own statements. Christian scholars have assumed from certain passages in the Gospels that he wished to give a new Torah to take the place of the Torah of Moses. How could he then have said explicitly that he comes only to fulfill it? But it is as I have said earlier: that the writer of the Gospels never meant to say that the Nazarene came to abolish Judaism but only that he came to establish a religion for the Gentiles from that time onward. Nor was it new, but actually ancient: [its commandments] being the Seven Commandments of the Sons of Noah, which were forgotten. The Apostles of the Nazarene then established them anew. However, those born as Jews, or circumcised as converts to Judaism ('The same law shall apply both for the native-born [Israelite] and for the proselyte that joins you'; Exodus 12:49) are obligated to observe all commandments of the Torah without exception.

But for the Gentiles he reserved the Seven Commandments which they have always been obligated to fulfill. It is for that reason that they were forbidden pollutions of idols, fornication, blood, and things strangled (Acts 15). They also forbade them circumcision and the Sabbath. All of this was in accord with the law and custom of our Torah, as expounded by our Sages, the true transmitters of Moses from Sinai. It was they who sat upon his seat (as the Nazarene himself attested; Mt. 23). It was they (the Sages or Pharisees) who said that it is forbidden to circumcise a Gentile who does not accept upon himself the yoke of all the commandments. The Sages likewise said that the Gentile is enjoined not to observe the Sabbath [fully]. The Apostles of the Nazarene therefore chose for those Gentiles who do not enter the Jewish faith that instead of circumcision they should practice immersion (for truly immersion is also a condition of full conversion) and a commemoration of the Sabbath was made for them on Sunday.

But the Nazarene and his Apostles observed the Sabbath and circumcision as mentioned earlier, for they were born as Jews. They observed the Torah fully, until after a period of time a few of them decided to give up the Torah among themselves completely. They said that its observance was too difficult for them and agreed to remove its yoke from their necks (Acts 15).

But even here they did correctly as far as the Gentiles were concerned, for they [the Gentiles] were not commanded to observe it. Nor is it proper to make it difficult for them, since they did not accept the Torah and are not enjoined to observe the 613 commandments. However, it is completely different as far as the Jews are concerned, for they became obligated to fulfill the Torah because God delivered them from the iron furnace (Egypt) to be the people of his possession. Therefore, they and their children became subject to it forever. This, their covenant, will not be forgotten by the Jewish people, nor be discontinued from their children. For it, they have given their lives throughout the generations, as the Psalmist has recorded, "All this has overtaken us. Yet we have not forgotten You, nor have we been false to Your covenant" (Psalms 44:18).

Certainly, therefore, there is no doubt that one who seeks truth will agree with our thesis, that the Nazarene and his Apostles never meant to abolish the Torah of Moses for one who was born a Jew. Likewise did Paul write in his letter to the Corinthians (1 Cor. 7), that each should adhere to the faith in which he was called. They therefore acted in accordance with the Torah by forbidding circumcision to Gentiles, according to the halachah, as it is forbidden to one who does not accept the yoke of the commandments. They knew that it would be too difficult for the Gentiles to observe the Torah of Moses. They therefore forbade them to circumcise, and it would suffice that they observe the Seven Noahide Commandments, as commanded to them through the halachah from Moses at Sinai.

It is therefore a habitual saying of mine (not as a hypocritical flatterer, God forbid, for I am of the faithful believers of Israel, and I know well that the remnant of Israel will not speak falsehood, nor will their mouths contain a deceitful tongue) that the Nazarene brought about a double kindness in the world. On the one hand, he strengthened the Torah of Moses majestically, as mentioned earlier, and not one of our Sages spoke out more emphatically concerning the immutability of the Torah. And, on the other hand, he did much good for the Gentiles — (provided they do not turn about his intent as they please, as some foolish ones have done because they did not fully understand the intent of the authors of the Gospels. I have recently seen someone publish a book, and he had no idea about what he was writing. For if he had understood the subject, he would have kept silent and not wasted the paper and ink. There are also found among us foolish scholars who know not their right from their left in the Written and Oral Torahs and cause the people to err with their pompous pronouncements. But there are true scholars among the Christians, just as there are the chosen few among Torah scholars; and there are few of the truly great.) — by doing away with idolatry and removing the images from their midst. He obligated them with the Seven Commandments so that they should not be as the beasts of the field. He bestowed upon them ethical ways, and in this respect he was much more stringent with them than the Torah of Moses, as is well-known. This in itself was most proper, as it is the correct way to acquire ethical practices, as the philosopher (Maimonides) mentioned. We have written similarly in our *siddur* [prayer book]. However, it is not necessary to impose upon Jews such extreme ethical practices, since they have been obligated to the yoke of Torah, which weakens the strength of the (evil) inclination without [these practices]. They have taken the oath at Sinai and are already trained in proper practice and nature. These are clear words that will not be rejected by a clear-thinking person.

If certain Christians who consider themselves scholars would understand this secret, who believe that they are commanded to abolish the Torah of Moses from the seed of Israel, they would not engage in such foolishness. The people listen to their self-conceived words, something which was never intended by the writers of the Gospels. Quite the opposite, they have written clearly that they intended the contrary.

Because of these errant scholars, hatred has increased towards the Jews who are blameless of any guilt and proceed innocently to observe their Torah with all their heart, imbued with the fear of God. They should instead bring their people to love the ancient Children of Israel who remain loyal to their God, as indeed commanded to Christians by their original teachers.

They even said to love one's enemies. How much more so to love us! In the name of heaven, we are your brothers! One God has created us all. Why should they abuse us because we are joined to the commandments of God, to which we are tied with the ropes of His love? We do this not to enjoy the pleasures of the (evil) inclination and the emptiness of a passing world. For truly, "We have become a byword among the nations" (Psalms 44), and with all this, "In God have we gloried all the day, and we will give thanks unto Your name forever" (ibid.). We pray for the good of the entire world, and especially for the benefit of these lands in which we reside, protecting us and our observance of the Torah...

You, members of the Christian faith, how good and pleasant it might be if you will observe that which was commanded to you by your first teachers; how wonderful is your share if you will assist the Jews in the observance of their Torah. You will truly receive reward as if you had fulfilled it yourselves — for the one who helps others to observe is greater than one who observes but does not help others to do so — even though you only observe the Seven Command-ments. I have written similarly in my pleasant work, *Torat Hakina'ot*: that the Jew who observes the Torah, but does not support it, is considered among the cursed; while the Gentile who does not observe the 613 commandments, but supports it, is considered among the blessed. [This letter was translated into English by Rabbi Harvey Falk, Brooklyn, New York, and published by *The Journal of Ecumenical Studies*, 19:1, Winter 1982.]

This is an example of how we are to view history through the light of Torah. On the one hand, Christianity was a tragedy of immense proportions for the Jewish nation. On the other hand, it served as a blessing for the many people who knew nothing of One God and the Seven Noahide commandments that are the basic commandments for all humanity. Unfortunately, many failed to understand its true message. This is another step in preparing the world for the Messianic Era which we will usher in, we hope, in the near future.

I conclude with an important statement by Maimonides (the Rambam) that was censored until just a few years ago. At the end of his *Mishneh Torah* (Code of Jewish Law), the Rambam writes:

The human mind cannot fathom the plan of the Creator, for God's ways and thoughts are not like ours (Isaiah 55:8). All these things concerning Jesus the Nazarene and [Mohammed] the Yishmaelite who arose after him, serve only to pave the way for the King Messiah who will perfect the entire world and bring all men to serve God together. It has thus been predicted, "I [God] will then transform all nations [by giving them] an evolved language, so that they may all call out in the Name of God and serve Him as one man" (Zephaniah 2:9).

How will this come about? The world is already permeated with ideas about the Messiah, the Torah and the Divine commandments. These ideas have already spread to the farthest corners of the world. Many nations have taken a serious interest in these matters. They engage in dialogues about the Torah's commandments. Some claim that they were to be taken literally [at one time], but today are abrogated. There are others who claim that they were never meant to be kept in the first place. They are just allegories with hidden meanings behind them, and that the Messiah has already come and revealed these hidden meanings. However, when the Messiah will truly come for all of human kind, and he will succeed in unifying humankind and bringing them to God and His Torah, then all will realize retroactively that they inherited misunderstandings and were misled by their leaders." (Laws of Kings, 11:4, M.S. Oxford Newbyer 568. Printed in *Sefer Asufot shel HaRambam*, Pardes, Israel).

37. The proper understanding of evolution is really the backbone of the holy Ari's writings. The Ari explains how each spiritual level is a denser manifestation of its (higher) predecessor, which then manifests itself in a denser form at the next level down, etc. This entire evolution proceeds from the highest spiritual level to the lowest and final physical state of manifestation. Then, after complete rectification is attained, the process is reversed. Everything is elevated from level to level to reconnect to its inner root on a higher level, thereby revealing a greater whole (see footnotes 6 and 7). Today, this elevation takes place only in the inner, not outer, mode (of physical reality). In the future, even the outer mode

will attain complete elevation. (See *Sha'ar Ma'amarei Rashbi* (Attieh edition), p. 38a top; (Ashlag edition), p. 180a bottom. See *Etz Chaim* 39:3, *Sha'ar Hamitzvot, Ekev* (Attieh edition), p. 41b; *Emek Hamelech, Sha'ar Olam Hatohu,* Chapter 31. For another approach regarding evolution from a Torah perspective, see David Sheinkin, M.D., *The Path of the Kabbalah.* See also Rabbi Abraham Isaac Kook (1865-1935), who wrote at a time when the belief in evolution was at its peak:

"The theory of evolution that is presently conquering the world, is compatible with the inner secrets of *Kabbalah* more than any other philosophy..." (*Orot Hakodesh,* p. 537).

Rabbi Kook was not suggesting that we are to accept the literal meaning of any scientific or philosophical doctrine. On the contrary, taken at surface value, the doctrine may seem strange, contradictory, or even heretical to the traditional Torah view of things. But the question remains: If all wisdom stems from one Source, why the disparity between Torah and Science? Why must the various theories of evolution contradict the Torah? Is there no correspondence?

Unquestionably, it is beyond our scope to deal fully with this subject, but this much can be said to explain what has been said so far and what will be said throughout this book and in the Epilogue:

From the moment Adam and Eve ate from the Tree of Knowledge, reality collapsed from a unified state (Tree of Life) into one of total fragmentation (Tree of Knowledge). This was the human counterpart to the first Shattering of the Vessels (which itself corresponds to the moment when the physical universe first came into being with a bang). At that moment, almost everything split apart, shifted downwards, shattered and broke. All of this was a preparation for the reality in which we now live, a reality in which the presence of God is completely undetectable. As a result, all Wisdom - including the Supernal Wisdom of the Torah - is in a state of exile, distortion and displacement. This is the state of the Tree of Knowledge, and later, the Second Tablets that were hewn by Moses after the First Tablets were "shattered." (See GRA, *Even Shleimah*, 8:26, footnote 22, pp. 83 (42a), 104 (52b). See Epilogue.

Kabbalah thus teaches that creation begins in a state of deficiency and must evolve upwards towards perfection. It is our job to mend the world and restore it to its inner source so that it will become unified with and correspond to its whole. In the final analysis, everything is part of this process of becoming complete and whole. As we have seen, the Ari uses three key words to describe this process: *Birrur* (Purification), *Tikun* (Rectification) and Aliyah (Elevation) of the entire universe. *Birrur* takes place by first breaking and removing the external shell or garment of Godlessness that keeps creation in its exiled, distorted state. Only then can we reconnect to the larger perspective and reawaken the inner spark of Godliness that lies hidden in every aspect of creation.

We do this by going into ourselves, looking out from a deeper level and seeing it from a greater perspective. Suddenly, a larger and new picture emerges and we see the correspondence and accordance of how the two pictures unite. This reveals the inner light. We then experience that the "whole is greater than the sum of its parts," that is the *"Partzuf,"* the greater gestalt of what is expressed in the Ari's *Kabbalah*.

We come back to the theory of evolution, which appears so antagonistic to religion and remains a thorn in the hearts of many traditional Jews. This indeed is paradoxical, for at its core the idea of evolution is not a contradiction to the Torah. On the contrary, it emanates from one of the highest sources of Supernal Light. The problem is that this Light is presently enclosed and trapped in a distorted state of exile which is its own outer shell!

Rabbi Abraham Isaac Kook referred to this inverse relationship between secular and spiritual wisdom:

Wherever heretics have gone astray, the true answer lies at hand. This applies not only to the text of the Torah (for which this rabbinic formula is generally applied), but also to emotional trends and intellectual movements. The selfsame arguments and lines of thought which lead to the denial of God will lead, if we search out their true origin and essence, to a higher form of faith than the simple conceptions that we entertained before the apparent breakdown. Thus, classical evolutionary theory, toward which all who follow a sense-based intellect now lean, seems at first to block off the light of a faith with a consciousness of the limitless power of God... However, once a thought-form of this kind makes its appearance in the intellect, though at first it may raise doubts and superficially drive the Divine light from the mind, it forms at a deeper level a most sublime basis on which to rest the concept of Divine Providence (*Orot Hakodesh*, p. 547).

The Divine Providence mentioned by Rabbi Kook is the force that guides history toward the ultimate reunification of all knowledge and wisdom: the Supernal Wisdom of the Torah of the Tree of Life. As this Wisdom manifests more in our generation, all the seemingly contradictory fragments of wisdom will fuse together and be understood from their higher root. The relationship between Torah and natural wisdom will be seen as very deep. In reality, one is an exact duplicate of the other, and they are both expressions of one unbroken continuum of wisdom coming from a higher dimension. See Rabbi Tzaddok HaCohen, *Dover Tzedek*, p. 194 (97d), where the author points out from the *Zohar* that each and every nation draw its wisdom from [a fragmented aspect of] the Garden of Eden.

38. *In Quantum Healing*, Deepak Chopra, M.D., also alludes to this understanding (see pp. 95-115, and particularly page 104).

39. See Epilogue, p. 170 and footnote 8.

40. The root of the word *lekabel* is shared by the word *hakbalah*, meaning a parallel, correspondence, or contrast and opposition. This is interesting because the soul of *Kabbalah* is to show the parallelism and correspondence between things. In *Kabbalah*, the opposite of something also shows unity because it is the other side of the same coin! Accordingly, when one "receives" from the "giver," he is corresponding and at the same time contrasting the giver. Thus, giving/receiving not only creates a contrast between giver and receiver; it also creates a parallelism. For the very act of receiving can then be transformed into giving. This giving can be expressed in passing on to someone else what I have received. Or it can be expressed in establishing a reciprocal union with the initial giver. Both are true, and one reinforces the other. *Kabbalah* is thus an appropriate name for the Wisdom that will help mankind overcome its selfishness and egoism.

41. The message of the New Age writings is universalism, unity, sharing [and thereby overcoming] differences, dialogue, etc. The corresponding technological aspects of these changes are seen most clearly in the area of telecommunication (comsat overseas television, telephone, computer modems and fax machines) which unites every point on the planet. This makes it possible for all to be in touch from the far corners of the globe and to correspond together at one center. In this way, the Messianic Light is being revealed a little bit at a time in a hidden manner. When the time comes, it will be revealed completely. This is the true "Messianic Conspiracy." See above, footnotes 5 and 6; see Epilogue.

42. The secret of paradox in *Kabbalah* is that even though, at first glance, two things may seem contradictory and antagonistic,

it is because they are being viewed separately as one against the other. However, when these same two things are viewed as complementary aspects of a dialectic (as two sides of the same coin), each reinforces the other to reveal a greater whole. The paradox is that this coin can only be seen from one side at a time! This is not because the greater whole is not understandable. Both sides of a dialectic can be held simultaneously in the mind's eye and understood very well. It is rather a problem of communication, of not being able to express both sides of a paradox at the same time. Put another way, the right half of our brain is capable of grasping the underlying unity behind two seemingly contradictory positions, but the right brain's grasp of the greater whole is necessarily non-verbal. The left brain, being verbal and descriptive, and using normal logic, can express what the right brain has grasped only as a paradox.

The ultimate paradox in Judaism is the existence of anything besides God. Judaism rests on the fact that God's Infinite Oneness is all that exists. The paradox involves God's infiniteness, on the one hand, and the finiteness of creation, on the other hand. In reality, infiniteness precludes the existence of finiteness. The same goes for God's Oneness as opposed to the inherent duality (multiplicity) of creation. How can we say that these seemingly incompatible realities are merely two sides of one coin?

See, however, Rabbi Meir ibn Gabbai, *Derech Emunah* [Kehot-Lubavitch (1988), p. 13; also quoted by the same author in his *Avodat Hakodesh*, Chelek Hayichud 8, p. 24 (12c)], quoting Rabbi Isaac the Blind:

The infinite light of God (*Ein Sof*) is an ongoing process of perfection without end. But if we assume that God's infiniteness precludes the possibility of finiteness, limitation, and constriction [i.e. that He cannot withhold Himself, on the one hand, or be more than what He is, on the other hand], we have diminished and taken away from His infinite perfection.

Rabbi Isaac the Blind is saying that God's infinite light must include both qualities because in essence they are one! Each side taken by itself is incomplete. Only together do they complement and complete each other, expressing the greater whole, the superposition that encompasses both in complete unity. This is truly an example of a mind-boggling paradox if we try to understand it as either this or that through the left brain alone. This is really a ground-and-figure relation-ship, each inclusively dependent on the other's existence!

For further reading, see the Ari, *Zohar HaRakiyah* (Sha'arei Ziv Institute), p. 23c; Ari and Rabbi Chaim Vital, *Likutim Chadashim* (Mevakshei Hashem Publications, Jerusalem, 1985), p. 17; "An Article of the Ari on the Theory of Tzimtzum-Constriction," Hebrew University Ms., Jerusalem, 8/417, printed by Gershon Sholem, "Writings of the Ari," p. 197; *Torat Shmuel*, Chabad, Mayim Rabim (Kehot-Lubavitch), p. 39; *D'rush Cheftzi Bah* (published with Simchat Cohen), printed under the name of Rabbi Chaim Vital but actually by Rabbi Yoseph ibn Tabul, p. 1c; Rabbi Abraham Isaac Kook, *Orot Hakodesh*, pp. 530-533. Note: In the writings of the Ari, the concept of *Tzimtzum* (self-constriction or self-limitation) is called *Ko'ach Hadin* (the power of restraint, the power of withholding, or the ability of a "vessel" to hold "light").

43. See the Radak's explanation of these verses.

ANNOTATOR'S EPILOGUE

PART I

Over seventy years ago, something strange happened in the physical sciences. Strange, astounding ideas about space and time, mind and matter, erupted in the scientific community. The theories of relativity and quantum physics, from which what is known as the "new physics" evolved, were suddenly inadequate. New ideas resulted in a radical change in how we are to view reality, an unexpected change that turns common sense upside down, distances us from materialism and establishes new relationships in consonance with mysticism.

Only in the last two decades, with the overflow of New Age books inspired by quantum physics and other sciences, with these books' relationship to eastern and western mysticism and their link to consciousness of reality, have the astonishing ideas expressed by the "new physics" gained the interest of laypersons, scholars and professionals alike.

Suddenly, different modes of wisdom are beginning to merge, establishing relationships unheard of before. We had been used to keeping each subject in its place, saying to ourselves, "Each subject bears no relationship to the other." We had created hard, absolute boundaries, determined that nothing new would invade our structured, personal wall.

Today, to the surprise of many, these walls have started to tumble down. Absolute boundaries are melting away, so much so that it isn't clear at deeper levels where one ends and the other begins. This, in essence, is a holistic message: On a deep level, there is an underlying unity running through the entire universe. That unity makes all wisdom merge into a gestalted tree, Wisdom. After all, isn't this what the new physics is trying to find, the "unified field theory" which reduces the four forces of nature into one underlying principle?

The fruits of this revolution are only now being plucked by philosophers and theologians. Many ordinary people, searching for a deeper meaning in their lives, are finding new insights for themselves and the world as a result of the new physics.

This astounding reformation supports universalism, holism, unity, and last but not least, the idea that the physical becomes a model to help us understand the spiritual, and vice versa. The question is: What is the meaning behind all this? Why is this happening? Looking into Kabbalah, particularly the ancient text of the Zohar attributed to the second-century sage Rabbi Shimon Bar Yochai, we see that these astounding developments — and their purpose — were prophesied in just a few sentences:

In the 600th year of the sixth millennium (5,600 of the Jewish calendar corresponding to 1840 C.E.), the gates of wisdom above (Kabbalah) together with the wellsprings of wisdom below (science) will open up, and the world will prepare to usher in the seventh millennium [the 7,000th year corresponding to the year 2240 C.E.] This is symbolized by a man who begins preparing to usher in the Sabbath on the afternoon of the sixth day. In the same way, toward the end of the sixth millennium, preparations are made for entering the seventh millennium. The Bible hints at this with the verse, "In the 600th year of Noah's life ... all the wellsprings of the great deep burst forth and the flood gates of the heaven were opened" (Genesis 7:11). Zohar, Vol. 1 (Vayeira), 117a.

Let us step back and examine this more deeply.

The Talmud (*Sanhedrin 97a, Rosh Hashanah 31a*) and the *Zohar* (2:176b) state that the first six days of creation as mentioned in Genesis correspond to 6,000 years. This symbolizes the time span of the universe as we know it. Just as the six days of creation (called work) symbolized time needed for the rectification and completion of God's world, the human race was given 6,000 years (corresponding to the six days of creation) in which to work, rectifying the universe, bringing it to a state of completion.

The seventh millennium (beginning with the year 6001) corresponds to the universe's Sabbath. That is, just as God rested on the seventh day of creation — a holy day symbolizing the completion of all creation, a time to reap and enjoy its fruit — so too the seventh millennium will usher in universal tranquility. God will reveal His presence with a magnitude that will unite with the whole universe, comparable to the union of husband and wife, a blissful state never known to mankind before (not even to Adam and Eve during their stay in the Garden of Eden). This glorious state defies description in human language. The best we can do is call it *Olam Haba*, the world to come, which begins at the seventh millennium (2240 C.E.), the universe's Great Sabbath."[1]

The period before that Sabbath is called the Messianic era. Corresponding to the last portion of the universe's "sixth day," it is a time when the whole world will become a "global village," when the Tree of Wisdom will flourish "like water that covers the sea." Everyone will experience, at his or her level, an aesthetic joy, a unity with all of creation and with God, who masterminded it all. We will see that all of humanity's wisdom are not only an expression of a unified wisdom, and not only an expression of themselves, but rather an expression of Divine, sublime existence, a unique oneness with the unified Light of God. Science will be revealed as a part of the Godly wisdom of Torah. Together with the Torah science will become a prism through which we will be able to *see the existence and unity of God*.[2] It is this unifying, sublime concept from which stems all aesthetic joy.

The period ushering in the Messianic era corresponds to the night, morning and afternoon of the sixth day of creation. Humanity now stands poised at the afternoon leading into the universe's Great Sabbath. We stand, as our sages described it, in the "foot steps of the Messiah."[3] If we are to view distant and current events through the light of Kabbalah, we will discover that events did not happen haphazardly, as it may appear on the surface. Through the light of Kabbalah, we will discover that there is an underlying, unifying system which ties historical events together, giving them meaning. Not surprisingly, the English word "history" is a play on the Hebrew word hester meaning hidden; that is, one has to look for the hidden factor to comprehend the world around us.

One of the main hidden factors behind historical events is the way in which these occurrences serve as a vehicle to unify all of creation and to reflect God's unity. Clandestinely, little by little, these occurrences are preparing the world for the Messianic era.

Our generation has witnessed an extraordinary awakening of inner spiritual wisdom. Any long-time student of Kabbalah can only be stunned by the recent proliferation of classical Kabbalah literature: in Hebrew, English and other languages. These texts continue to increase the universe's spiritual momentum. Consequently, the flood gates of heaven have opened.

The revelations of the last two centuries are well-known but nonetheless astonishing. Stimulated by the eighteenth century's Industrial Revolution, many new theories and technologies burst forth with such intensity that a total new paradigm of scientific thought and consciousness emerged. Electromagnetic theory emerged midway through the nineteenth century. This paved the way for the invention of radio waves, telecommunication, television and computers, not to mention new psychological, neurological descriptions of the brain, black hole phenomena and quantum mechanics, which is the fundamental underpinning of all modern sciences. Nuclear power, laser beams, space travel, molecular biology, DNA, genetic engineering and the holographic model are a few more examples of twentieth century scientific discoveries, discoveries that have given us completely new ways to perceive and appreciate our world.

Perhaps of even greater significance has been the effect of nineteenth century breakthroughs in non-euclidian geometry. They set the stage for the emergence of Einsteinian relativity, quantum theory and today's search for the Unified Field Theory. Currently dubbed "Super Strings," the Unified Field Theory is, according to today's leading physicists, an unmistakable genesis of a new physics, one which speaks in terms of ten and 26 dimensions. Anyone who has ever heard of *Kabbalah* will know what these numbers signify.

These are the "sparks" of the Messianic era, each one popping forth at its proper time, bringing forth those historical breakthroughs and increasing the momentum toward the Great Sabbath. Each new scientific revelation clarifies ideas expressed in *Kabbalah*, resulting in a demystification of *Kabbalah* and, in turn, of science. In other words, science's newly discovered models and metaphors (its external wisdom) will help illuminate the secret, ancient mysteries of *Kabbalah*. Reciprocally, Kabbalah's ancient mysteries (its internal wisdom) will define, explain and help reshape our perception of the entire physical world.

It is now clear that we are witnessing the fulfillment of the Zohar's prophecy: that from 1840 C.E. (5,600 in the Jewish calendar) and onwards, "the floodgates of heaven will open." What does this mean? Simply that the inner wisdom of Torah-*Kabbalah* will merge with the "wellsprings from below" (i.e., science). Why? To "prepare the world," as the *Zohar* puts it, enabling it to see God's unity and presence in every minor detail of our lives. The *Zohar* elaborates that the purpose of the Messianic era is to prepare the universe for the Great Sabbath. In other words, the *Zohar* is asserting that the revelation of new sciences and technology plays a role in the Messianic process.

It is worth mentioning that this notion of the confluence of *Kabbalah* and science is discussed at length by the Vilna Gaon, the Torah luminary of the seventeenth century in the book entitled

Kol Hator (The Voice of the Turtle Dove). A collection of teachings about the Final Redemption, *Kol Hator* was transcribed by one of the Vilna Gaon's disciples, Rabbi Hillel Rivlin of Schklov. In the chapter entitled Sha'ar Be'er Sheva (Gate of the Well of the Seven [Wisdom]),[4] Rabbi Hillel writes in the name of his master:

The wisdom of Torah is contained in the light of supernal wisdom. In order to grasp this wisdom, however, it is also necessary to learn the seven wisdom that are hidden in external reality, the dimension of Nature. This is the mystery of ... "they stood on the bottom side of the mountain (Exodus 19:17) [the verse that refers to the nation of Israel receiving the Torah at Mount Sinai]. [The intention here is that reality consists of two sides: a spiritual "top side" and a physical "bottom side."] Our Master said that usage of patterns and examples in the bottom side of reality is analogous to a teacher of children who is able to explain numerous matters in Torah (that his young pupils might not otherwise understand) by using toy models ... as well as simple diagrams (Paragraph 6).

According to the Vilna Gaon, the "top side" of reality corresponds to the "gates of wisdom from above." The "bottom side" corresponds to the "wellsprings of wisdom below." These two "sides" must be joined. The first step toward this end is to use the most basic models of physical reality in order to understand the most basic spiritual truths. More advanced steps involve the utilization of science's most sophisticated models, paradigms and metaphors in order to understand the Torah's loftiest teachings: the *Kabbalah*. Only then can the Kabbalah's wisdom reconnect us to the underlying unity of all scientific knowledge, showing us how physical reality is no less of a divine revelation than the Torah itself.

This symbiosis is a universal factor in logic, not unique to the Vilna Gaon. For example, Concept A may use Concept B to explain Concept A, or vice versa; and the two may merge into a more encompassing, fused comprehension. Rabbi Nachman of Breslov expresses the same idea in another context:

We know from experience that it is impossible to perceive a deep concept without seeing it first through a simple understand-able context, so that the lofty concept can then be easily understood (*Likutei Moharon*, 1:30:1).

We see that this holds true everywhere: that the outer or simple idea is used to express a more refined concept, clothed in a simple idea, like an analogy, to enable others to comprehend the refined concept.

The Vilna Gaon's disciple continues:

There's no other avenue to attain this ascendancy except extensive, well-founded training in both ex-tremities, i.e., the depths of the earth (science) and the heights of the heavens (*Kabbalah*). This is the intention of the verse, "Only to you, O God, can be ascribed greatness and power, harmony and eternity, splendor and all that binds heaven and earth (1 Chronicles 29:11). "We must be *well versed in our Torah's secrets*, derived from Supernal Wisdom. And we must be equally well-versed in the secret depths of the laws of nature that derive from the wisdom of Torah. These two extremities are interdependent, as indicated in the statement of the holy *Zohar*: "In the 600th year of the sixth millennium, the gates of wisdom above together with the wellsprings of wisdom below will open up and the world will prepare to usher in the seventh millennium." (Paragraph 10)

On the basis of a number of scriptural verses men-tioned above, we explained that the revelation of the underlying principles of the (seven) wisdom is depen-dent on the rebuilding of Jerusalem, the ingathering of the exiles and the reflourishing of the Holy Land. An oft repeated expression of my master was, "*To the extent that one lacks knowledge of the properties of the natural sciences, he will lack one hundred-fold in the wisdom of the Torah. And to the extent that the Torah sages attain (knowledge of) the underlying principles of the properties of nature, they will increase (their understanding of) the wisdom of Torah one hundred-fold."[5]* (This confluence, however, is dependent on the Jewish's nation's return to the land of Israel.) (Paragraph 12)

That oft-repeated expression, "to the extent that one lacks knowledge of the properties of the natural sciences," etc., was expressed conversely on purpose. The intention of the full statement becomes clear when we remember that throughout *Kol Hator,* the "Wisdom of the Torah" refers primarily to its esoteric teachings, the *Kabbalah.* (See previous paragraph #10.) It is significant that the Vilna Gaon speaks here of "one hundred gates of wisdom" while the *Zohar's* statement refers to the "gates of wisdom above" opening together with the "gates of wisdom below." The apparent repetition of the Vilna Gaon's statement[7] can now be understood, in the context of the *Zohar,* as a reference to the interdependence of science and *Kabbalah.* These two bodies of knowledge are really two sides of the same coin, two aspects of something greater. When we will no longer view them as opposing disciplines, our understanding of both will change radically.

The present Torah analogizes the supernal wisdom in the spiritual dimension and science analogizes the supernal wisdom in the physical dimension. *Together* they embody the higher unity of Supernal Wisdom: the Torah of the future. This, of course, will give us a new meta-understanding of the reflection of God's unity in all creation, known in *Kabbalah* as the hidden light.

This is the universal purpose of fulfilling the Messianic destiny and serving to guide and prepare all humanity for a major shift in consciousness.

PART II

Originally, the Supernal Wisdom of all which was, is and will be was identified in the Garden of Eden as the Tree of Life and the Tree of Joining Knowledge of Good and Potential Evil.[8] All this is called Torah, meaning teachings of Supernal Wisdom. Adam and Eve sinned when they "ate" from the Tree of Joining Knowledge, for they were supposed to sustain themselves with fruits from the Tree of Life. Consequently, the Tree of Joining Knowledge split away from the Tree of Life, all of Wisdom shattered and therefore Knowledge of reality plummeted. The fragments of Knowledge scattered to the four corners of the globe, and each nation took a piece for itself.

Ever since, no body of wisdom has been complete, for it needs its missing parts. This is called the "exiled state," meaning that everything carries a certain percent of distortion. This includes the classical Torah because it too is in exile. Therefore, at first glance, one cannot really understand the Torah's precise meaning. One must clarify a great deal before one can digest its fruit.

The Vilna Gaon explains this concept of the Torah in exile:

On the surface, the Aggadot (expositions of the rabbis) appear as wasted expressions, God forbid. Yet all the secrets of the universe are concealed within them. This is alluded to in the verse, "And he is afflicted because of our sins" (Isaiah 53:5). According to the Talmud (Sotah 14a), this passage refers to Moses, who sinned by hitting a rock to obtain water instead of

135

asking the rock to give water (Numbers 20). The "hitting" represents the extra effort one has to expend to understand Torah, often compared to life-giving water. Because of Moses' anger, it was decreed that his holy teachings would be hidden in abstractions, such as *Aggadot*, these strange-sounding expositions of the rabbis, rather than being clearly evident. This, in turn, would make it possible for the scoffers of each generation to belittle those teachings. Moses pleaded with God not to conceal the Torah's secrets but his request was not granted. The same is true concerning Moses' death and his burial outside the land of Israel. He pleaded to enter the land but his request was not granted. [In all these cases, the intention is that the Torah's secrets would be exiled, clothed in garments unbefitting their sanctity.] In the Messianic era, however, the hidden secrets of Moses' Torah will be redeemed, and that which was obscured will instead be obvious. This is the new Torah to be revealed in the future (*Even Shleimah*, 8:26 p. 42a (83), footnote 22, commentary to the *Heichalot Pekudei*, p. 28d).

From here, we learn that the metaphor of the Torah being clothed in garments not befitting its sanctity indicates the need to conceal the truth from those who would misuse it. This idea is expressed allegorically in another *Midrash*: At the time of creation, the fruit trees refused to produce edible bark and rinds. Instead, they enclosed their fruits in inedible shells to protect themselves against inconsiderate people who might eat the entire tree! In a similar way, the symbolic garments serve to protect the Torah while they simultaneously disgrace it.

Actually, the concept of the Torah in exile is already discussed in the Talmud itself (*Chullin* 60b): Rabbi Shimon Ben Lakish said, "There are many verses in the Torah which, at first glance, ought to be burned like the books of the heretics, but they are really the very essence of the Torah." (This is in order to conceal the truth from one who is not yet ready for it. This is the Torah in exile.)

The master Kabbalist Rabbi Shlomo Eliyashiv clarifies this concept:

[As a consequence of Adam's eating from the Tree of Knowledge,] the external forces now have control over the emanations of the light of knowledge that descend below. This is the exile of the Torah. As a result, the Torah has become clothed in foreign garments and in shells of concealment that are not befitting or comely to her as, for example, the section at the end of Vayishlach: "These are the kings that reigned in the land of *Edom...*" (Genesis 36:31-39). (This paragraph contains the foundations for the Zohar's "Book of Concealment" and the basis for most of Lurianic *Kabbalah*.) This is also true of many sections of the written Torah (the Bible) as well as other similar passages discussed in the Talmud (*Chullin* 60b) where entire sentences appear superfluous. Similarly, there are numerous expositions of the sages which are difficult even to listen to and one's sensibilities are astounded by them. Yet the secrets of the Torah and the universe are hidden within them. This is all due to the emanations of the light of the Tree of Knowledge, clothed in external forces' shells of concealment. Hence, the exiles of the Divine presence, the people of Israel and the Torah are all due to Adam's eating from the Tree of Knowledge (*Leshem Sh'vo V'achlamah, De'ah* Vol. 2 p. 89 (177) and p. 153 (305b)).

In the end, the Torah will shine forth in all its supernal radiance, but in the meantime it is in exile. Nevertheless, the very shells that surround and camouflage the Torah allow it to infiltrate into places it might not have reached.

It is interesting to reexamine the Vilna Gaon's statement that the "bottom side" of Mount Sinai alludes to "the wellsprings of wisdom below," that is, the natural sciences which are the wisdom of physical reality. When Moses came down from the mountain and witnessed the sin of the Golden Calf, he broke the first tablets in which are contained the secrets of the universe, the esoteric Torah. The Torah's exact words are, "He broke them on the bottom side of the mountain" (Exodus 32:19). This intimates that the esoteric teachings had to go into exile, to the bottom - earthly — side of reality. The Torah's exile is thus God's disguised way of bringing back all the fragmented sparks of His Supernal Wisdom.

Everything, however tiny and trivial it may seem to us, is very important to God. It is all being retrieved, reprocessed and transformed back into the Supernal Wisdom. This explains many phenomena, including the fact that science and *Kabbalah* are coming together. Very simply, science is returning to its source of Supernal wisdom. This also explains why everything looks so fragmented, why we need information even from far out places in order to get a clearer picture.[9]

This is what is known in the *Zohar* and Lurianic *Kabbalah* as the elevation of the scattered sparks to create a gestalt called a *Partzuf*.[10] In modern terms, this is known as the whole being greater than the sum of its parts.[11] One always has to be open-minded, careful never to think, "Oh, I've got the whole picture," or "I have the ultimate truth of the matter and that's that." Whatever we have, know and see as a whole, is in essence always part of a greater whole!

Secondly, we are not sure if we have all the parts. Yesterday we were partially right, today a little more and tomorrow still more correct. All this is saying that the world is being led back, step by step, to become whole and to continue where Adam and Eve left off. This is the purpose of the Messianic era, when the whole universe will reveal itself as a reflection of God's unity. It is through this medium that mankind will cleave to the oneness of God.

In closing, I would like to introduce an illustration of a Torah-science relationship. *Kabbalah* has many branches and so does science. The different sciences can help explain or parallel different parts of Kabbalah and vice versa. I chose here to use an idea of quantum theory because the ignited spark of holiness which lies within it can serve as one of the most important fundamentals and prerequisities for an understanding of Kabbalah in our lives in a very deep and mature manner. What we can learn from this is enormous.

The Torah tells us, "You should know (conceptually) to this day and bring it down (clearly) to your innermost heart that the Lord (YHVH) is God (Elokim) in the heavens above and on the earth below; there is nothing else" (Deuteronomy 4:39).

The narrative states that God's unity refers not only to the oneness of rule (there are no other gods) and not only to the uniqueness of His Oneness (there is no other oneness like it), but that He is all there is. That is, the belief that God is One means that, in spite of all the evidence of diversity and separateness in the universe, all there is in reality is God's absolute and indivisible unity. From the divine view of creation, there is no finite and objective universe that exists as some kind of independent substance "out there" whose essence separates and interposes God from Himself (God forbid!). Even though we feel ourselves and sense the world around us as "solid, hard reality," utterly distinct from our concept of godliness, Jewish tradition teaches that this is only how it appears from one perspective.

From another perspective, we are only like the rays of the sun in the sun itself, and if God were to remove his vitality for even one moment, all reality — the multifarious rays of life — would revert back to absolute Nothingness! It is only because of God's decrees that the world appears the way it does and operates according to physical laws and spiritual ordinances. Thus, reversing our intuitive assumption of what is "real" and what is not, only God's all-pervading unity can be said to be truly real and all that there is.[12]

Rabbi Moshe Ben-Yehudah

EPILOGUE FOOTNOTES

1. We are now in the year 5,753, corresponding to 1992-1993 C.E. *Rosh Hashanah*, the Jewish New Year, normally takes place in September. This past *Rosh Hashanah* commemorates 5,753 years since the creation of Adam and Eve.

2. It is important to note here that this statement is the key to determining when wisdom becomes part of Torah and when it does not. It is a relative concept, depending on whether one understands wisdom for its own sake or sees through it the unity of God or other Torah concepts. In his book *Adir Bamarom*, the Ramchal clarifies this point:

    When our Sages dealt with astronomical or scientific matters concerning the sun and the stars, etc., they spoke mainly from the "inner level." From this inner point of view, the knowledge of the Torah encompasses all wisdoms. But this is only true from the "inner mode" of creation. In the "external mode" of creation, all these matters have nothing to do with Torah (insofar as they are concerned only with their own existence and not with the existence and unity of God). The Torah is never concerned with external phenomena as such, except with regards to the fulfillment of the commandments (which themselves point to the existence and unity of God). In this sense, Torah is Torah and anything outside of Torah (which is from the point of view of the "outer mode" is self-evident for its own sake) isn't Torah.

However, from the point of view of the "inner mode" of the Torah, all phenomena is Torah (because the inner mode always points to God's sublime unity). Therefore, since the wisdoms of science normally deal with the outer mode alone, they are not Torah (because their purpose is generally for their own sake, which stems from the outer mode) (new edition, p. 236; old edition, p. 133 (67a)).

The implication is that if a person understands science through the inner mode (and this can only be done through *Kabbalah*, to show God's unity, etc.), *then science is considered part of the inner mode, and learning it is considered part of one's Torah.* (See footnote 7. See also Rabbi Tzaddok HaCohen of Lublin, *Likutei Ma'amarim*, pp. 42a, 58a. See *Midrash Shmuel* on *Avot* 2:16.)

3. We are now in the early afternoon of this cosmic sixth day. "Morning" began in the year 5,500 (1740 C.E.) and the year 5,750 (1990) marks the noon hour! The equation is simple: one thousand years is a day based on Psalm 90:4: "Indeed a thousand years are in your eyes like a yesterday that has passed like a watch of the night." The first 500 years is night and the second 500 years is day. Therefore you divide twelve hours of daylight into 500. The result is 41 years and eight months, one "cosmic hour" (see *Pirkei Rabbi Eliezer*, Chapt. 48, Sanhedrin 38a). Over six hours have passed since the dawn of 1740 C.E. Since we are in the seventh hour of the sixth day, our calculation is $(41 + 8/12) \times 6 = 250$ years. Then $1740 + 250 = 1990$ or, in the Jewish calendar, $5,500 + 250 = 5,750$.

4. The original text of *Kol Hator* appears only in the original manuscript, kept for over 200 years by the Rivlin family,

descendants of Rabbi Hillel with the advice of the great Kabbalists of Jerusalem, decided to publish a condensed version of this lengthy and difficult treatise, keeping the terminology as simple as possible so that it could be studied by non-Kabbalists, too. Therefore, the printed *Kol Hator* is not in the author's original words. In 1968, it was printed again by two different editors: Rabbi Menachem Kasher and the Va'ad (Council) of Dissemination of *Kol Hator*, Bnei Brak. To date, only the Bnei Brak edition contains Sha'ar Be'er Sheva (The Gate of the Seven Wisdoms), the chapter on the confluence of *Kabbalah* and science. Since the Bnei Brak edition has been out of print for over twenty years, this lost doctrine of the Vilna Gaon went unnoticed by scholars and the general public. Some traditional scholars challenged its authenticity, saying "The Vilna Gaon wouldn't say such strange things," etc. In retrospect, however, we see that these words mirror historical and current events. This fact and others beyond the scope of this book, confirm that the Vilna Gaon actually dictated these teachings to Rabbi Hillel.

5. This statement is referring particularly to *Kabbalah* and to small areas of the revealed Torah. For most areas in the revealed Torah, the study of science and other wisdoms is unnecessary. This clarifies the misunderstandings many people seem to encounter when interpreting the Vilna Gaon's words as a reference mainly to the revealed Torah. It is explicit in *Kol Hator* that this statement refers mainly to *Kabbalah*. For example, see *Sha'ar Be'er Sheva*, paragraph 10, where Rabbi Hillel writes, "We must be well versed in the secrets of our Torah."

It is significant to note that this statement is also recorded in the Vilna Gaon's name by Rabbi Boruch Shick in the introduction to his translation of Euclid's Geometry, printed in Amsterdam in 1780, under the Vilna Gaon's auspices. He quotes this statement that he heard himself from the Vilna Gaon's mouth in January 1778.

6. In the original text, this sentence does not appear here. In context, however, the implication is clear. Paragraph 12 can be divided into three parts: 1) The revelation of the underlying principle of "secular" wisdom, i.e., the "opening of the wellsprings of wisdom below," depends on the return of the Jewish nation to the land of Israel. 2) These two factors together will make it possible to understand the wisdom of the Torah one hundred-fold, i.e., "the opening of the gates of wisdom from above." 3) The revelation of the confluence between Torah (*Kabbalah*) and science depends again on the return of the Jewish nation to the land of Israel. This reading is further supported by Rabbi Hillel's statement (in paragraph #14): "On a number of occasions our master (the Vilna Gaon) told us that the most opportune place for attaining 'the gates of wisdom above the wellsprings of wisdom below' is the holy city of Jerusalem may it be rebuilt and established."

7. The Vilna Gaon's statement regarding the role of secular knowledge in helping to uncover Judaism's secrets of esoteric wisdom is almost unheard of in traditional rabbinic literature. One of the few exceptions is a text that appears in the writings of Rabbi Moshe Chaim Luzzatto (the Ramchal). Commenting on the Zohar's requirement "to know the structure of the human body and to look into the world in order to attain knowledge of the divine," he explains that the human body (the microcosm) and the universe (the macrocosm) are physical counterparts of spiritual processes. It is therefore necessary to study their structure and dynamics on a material plane in order to gain a deeper understanding of the divine process itself.

    Two parallel texts (with slight variations) appear in the Ramchal's introduction to *Adir Bamarom* and at the end of *Milchemet Moshe* (printed as an appendix to *Da'at Tevunot*, B'nei Brak, 1975). After explaining the Zohar's first three categories, he writes:

The fourth category of knowledge is to know the mystery of this world, as the *Zohar* states, "to look into the world." This means that there is an obligation to know that everything in this world operates according to the mystery of the *Sefirot*, that is, to know the internal design that is imminent in nature. This is the intention of the numerical equivalency between the word Nature (*Hateva* = 86) and God (*Elokim* = 86). This is in contrast to the opinion of the philosophers (who comprehend the world solely as it appears to their senses). The truth is, however, that the laws governing the existence of every creature in the world can only be understood in terms of the *Sefirot*. The knowledge of natural science as well as all other knowledge is predicated upon this principle, i.e., the mystery of the *Sefirot* according to their true supernal function.

One must then know the root of all this. Concerning the (second category of) knowledge of the human body we have explained the principle that "from my flesh (microcosms) I will behold God (macrocosm)" (Job 19:26). This same principle is to be applied to the knowledge of nature and its laws.

Thus there are things that can only be understood about the *Sefirot* via a knowledge of the human body, while there are other things that can only be understood about the *Sefirot* via a knowledge of the world. Although both of these really constitute one unified system, certain things are revealed in man and others are revealed in the world.

It follows that the world must be understood in two (complementary) ways: First, in its manifestation here below. This can only be done, however, if one concentrates on the deeper *sefirotic* design that is inherent in the world, as opposed to the cynicism of the philosophers. It is around this principle that the majority of the Sages' aggadic and *midrashic* statements revolve when they speak about ma'aseh *Bereishit* (the World's Creation) and other matters relating to heaven and earth. This knowledge is also exceedingly great and precious. Second, after a proper understanding of the laws of nature has been established below, their mystery and root must be ascertained above in the Sefirot. Only then can we understand the why of things. Lastly, we must understand all of this within the Torah's secrets, for all of these matters are contained within its teachings.

In his Ma'amar HaAggadot (printed at the beginning of all editions of Ein Yaakov), the Ramchal further clarifies how the Talmudic Sages related to the "external" wisdom of the world:

The Sages encoded much of the esoteric tradition that they had received concerning nature or astronomy. In other words, they utilized the knowledge of nature and astronomy accepted among gentile scholars of their time to transmit something else. Thus, they never intended to teach the physical "facts" concerning these phenomena but, rather, to utilize these facts as vehicles for Kabbalistic secrets. Therefore, one should not think that they were wrong because a particular [scientific] model they used is no longer accepted. Their intention was to clothe the hidden tradition in the accepted knowledge of their generation. That very tradition could have been clothed in a different garment according to what was accepted [as a scientific fact] in other generations. And, in fact, the originator of that particular aggadic statement would have done so himself if he would have expressed it in another generation.

In Adir Bamarom (p. 66b, new edition, p. 235), the Ramchal writes further:

All the Sages' aggadic statements concerning the sun and the other stars that are no longer accepted [according to modern science] are referring to the inner dimension of Divine Providence. One who is not familiar with the Paths of Wisdom (Kabbalah) can only grasp the external structure of reality in accordance with its physical description. . . The essence of the matter is that the Sages are referring to the inner structure of reality. This is the knowledge of the Torah, which encompasses all wisdom. It is, however, all in the mystery of the internal design and not in the external form.

Last, but not least, the present Lubavitcher Rebbe said, "The truest unification between Torah and Science is such that, from [Science's] theoretical models, it is possible to perceive matters pertaining to the innermost aspects of Torah" ("Concerning the Development of Science in Our Time," printed in Hebrew translation from "Talks in Yiddish," Sect. *Miketz* and *Mishpatim*, 1976-1977, in *B'Or HaTorah*, Vol. 2, pg. 8).

8. See *The Path of the Kabbalah* by Dr. David Sheinkin, pg. 116. The root of evil is based on separateness and concealment from the greater whole. (On this level, it is not evil yet. Evil is only when it has the inverse negative effect.) The greater whole here is the union of the two trees. See *Leshem Sh'vo V'achlamah, De'ah*, Vol. 2, pg. 42 (83). Note that an anagram for the word "evil" is "veil," which is concealment and separation.

9. In the Ari's Lurianic *Kabbalah*, this process is called *Birrur*, purification. This is the step before rectification. See Chagigah 5b: "God cries over the pride and glory of Israel which was removed at the time of the destruction of the Temple and given over to the nations of the world" until the redemption. The Talmud continues: "Since [the Jews] were exiled, there was no greater loss of the Torah." The loss of Torah is that it goes into hiding among the nations of the world. See the Ari, z"l (z"l is an acronym of zichrono livracha, may his memory be blessed). *Sha'ar Hakavanot*, pg. 58b and *Sha'ar Ruach Hakodesh*, pg. 5b (Rashi print): "From the time the Torah was burned, her secrets and inner secrets were given over to the outside forces. This is called the Torah in

exile." See Vilna Gaon, *Even Shleimah*, page 52b, notes. See *Likutei Moranan* of Rabbi Nachman of Breslov, Vol. 1:56:4: "In very low places are hidden very high esoteric Torah."

10. See footnote 2 in this book. This is to view it "all" as one gestalted whole. There is something in the whole which is not in the sum of its parts. See next note.

11. This statement is actually made by the Ramchal (Rabbi Moshe Chaim Luzzatto) in this *Book of Logic (Sefer Higayon)*, Chapter 10. This is the meaning of a *Partzuf* in the writings of the Ari. This is the theme which runs throughout this entire book.

12. See *Nefesh Hachaim* by Rabbi Chaim Volozhin, Gate 3. See *Tanya* (Chabad) by Rabbi Shneur Zalman of Liadi, *Sha'ar Yichud V'emunah*, Chapter 6.

BIBLIOGRAPHY

Ashlag, Yehuda L. *A Study of the Kabbalah*. Jerusalem: Yeshivat Kol Yehuda.

Ashlag, Yehuda L. *Kabbalah, Ten Luminous Emanations*. Jerusalem: Research Center of *Kabbalah*, 1973.

Barnett, Lincoln. *The Universe and Dr. Einstein*. New York: Bantam, 1979 (12th printing), William Morrow, 1948.

Bateson, Gregory. *Mind and Nature, A Necessary Unity*. New York: E. P. Dutton, 1979.

Berg, Phillip S. *The Kabbalah Connection*. Jerusalem: Research Center of *Kabbalah*, 1983.

Bentov, Itzhak. *With Mirtala — A Cosmic Book*. Rochester, Vermont: Inner Traditions, Ltd., Destiny Books, 1988.

Capra, Fritjof. *The Tao of Physics*. Berkeley: Shambhala Press, 1975.

Capra, Fritjof. *The Turning Point: Science, Society, and the Rising Culture*. New York: Simon and Schuster, 1982.

Chopra, Deepak. *Quantum Healing*. New York: Bantam, 1989.

Davies, Paul. *The Cosmic Blueprint*. New York: Simon and Schuster, 1989.

Dobin, Joel C. *The Astrological Secrets of the Hebrew Sages*. New York: Inner Traditions, Ltd., 1977.

Falk, Harvey. "Rabbi Jacob Emden's Views on Christianity." *The*

Journal of Ecumenical Studies, 19:1, Winter 1982.

Franck, Adolphe. *The Kabbalah*. Secaucus, N.J.: Citadel Press, 1967.

Fuller, J.F.C. *The Secret Wisdom of the Qabalah - A Study in Jewish Mystical Thought*. London: Rider & Company.

Goodwin Jocelyn, *Harmonies of Heaven and Earth*. Rochester, Vermont: Inner Traditions, Ltd., 1987.

Halevi, Z'ev ben Shimon. *A Kabbalistic Universe*. York Beach, Maine: Samuel Weiser, Inc., 1977.

Halevi, Z'ev ben Shimon. *The Anatomy of Fate*. Bath, England: Gateway Books, 1978.

Halevi, Z'ev ben Shimon. *Tree of Life*. London: Rider & Company, 1972.

Halevi, Z'ev ben Shimon. *Kabbalah and Exodus*. York Beach, Maine: Samuel Weiser Inc., 1988.

Halevi, Z'ev ben Shimon. *Kabbalah, Tradition of Hidden Knowledge*. London: Thames and Hudson, 1979.

Halevi, Z'ev ben Shimon. *Kabbalah and Psychology*. Bath, England: Gateway Books, 1986.

Hall, Manly P. *The Secret Teachings of All Ages*. Los Angeles: The Philosophical Research Society, Inc., 1977.

Heline, Corine. *The Bible and the Tarot*. California: De Vorss & Co., 1969.

Johnson, Paul. *History of the Jews*. New York: Harper & Row, 1987.

Johnson, Ken. *The Ancient Magic of the Pyramids*. New York: Simon & Schuster, 1977.

Kalish, Isidore. *Sepher Yetzirah - A Book on Creation, or, Jewish Metaphysics of Remote Antiquity*. L. H. Frank & Co., 1877 (Reprinted by A.M.O.R.C.).

Kaplan, Aryeh. *The Handbook of Jewish Thought*. New York: Moznaim, 1979.

Kaplan, Aryeh. *Inner Space*. New York: Moznaim, 1990.

Kaplan, Aryeh. *Meditation and Kabbalah*. New York: Samuel Weiser, Inc., 1986.

Kook, Abraham I. *Derech Hatechiyah*. In Payne, Richard J. (ed.) *The Classics of Western Spirituality*. New York: Paulist Press, 1978.

Kook, Abraham I. *Orot Hakodesh*. Jerusalem: Mossad HaRav Kook, 1963-64.

Krakovsky, Levi I. *Kabbalah — The Light of Redemption*. Brooklyn, NY: The Kabbalah Foundation, 1950.

Krakovsky, Levi I. *The Kabbalah: A Preface to The Zohar*. Jerusalem: Publisher withheld by author.

Lovelock, J.E. *Gaia — A New Look At Life On Earth*. New York: Oxford University Press, 1979.

Luzzatto, Moshe Chaim. *Derech Hashem (The Way of God)*. New York: Feldheim, 1983.

Mascaro, Juan. *The Dhammapada* (translation). London: Penguin Books, 1973.

Mascaro, Juan. *The Upanishads* (translation). London: Penguin Books, 1965.

McClain, Ernest G. *The Pythagorian Plato - Prelude to the Song Itself*, York Beach, Maine: Nicolas-Hayes, Inc., 1978.

Newman, Louis I. *The Hasidic Anthology*. New York: Schocken Books, 1963.

Nightingale, Florence. *Letters From Egypt, A Journey on the Nile*. London: Weidenfeld & Nicolson, reprinting of Barrie & Jenkins, Ltd., 1887.

Ponce, Charles. *Kabbalah — An Introduction and Illumination For The World Today*. San Francisco: Straight Arrow Books, 1973.

Prigogine, Ilya and Stengers, Isabelle. *Order Out of Chaos: Man's New Dialogue with Nature*. New York: Bantam, 1984.

Roth, Cecil. *A History of the Jews*. New York: Schocken Books, 1961.

Schaya, Leo. *The Universal Meaning of The Kabbalah*. Baltimore: Penguin Books, Inc., 1958.

Scholem, Gershon G. *Kabbalah*. New York: New American Library, 1978.

Scholem, Gershon G. *Zohar - The Book of Splendor*. New York: Schocken Books, 1967.

Schuon, Frithjof. *The Transcendant Unity of Religions*. Wheaton, IL: The Theosophical Publishing House, 1970.

Smith, Huston. *Forgotten Truth*. New York: Harper & Row, 1985.

Steinsaltz, Adin. *The Thirteen Petalled Rose*. New York: Basic Books, 1980.

Suars, Carlo. *The Sepher Yetzira - Including the Original Astrology to the Qabala and its Zodiac*. Boston: Shambhala Press, 1976.

Suars, Carlo. *The Qabala Trilogy - The Cipher of Genesis; The Song of Songs; The Sepher Yetzira*. Boston: Shambhala Press, 1985.

The Three Initiates - The Kybalion - Hermetic Philosophy. Chicago: The Yogi Publication Society, 1912.

Tillich, Paul. *The Dynamics of Faith*. New York: Harper & Row, 1957.

Waite, A. E. *The Holy Kabbalah*. New York: University Books, 1960.

Wilbur, Ken. *Up From Eden - A Transpersonal View of Human Evolution*. Boston: Shambhala Press, 1986.

Wilhelm, Richard. *The Secret of the Golden Flower — A Chinese Book of Life*. New York: Harcourt Brace Jovanich, 1931.

Wilson, Ian. *Exodus: The True Story Behind the Biblical Account*. New York: Harper & Row, 1985.

INDEX

Eliyashiv, Shlomo, 137
Enoch, 61, 65
Eshet Chayil, 75-76, 79-86,
87-89
Esther, 80
Eve, 80, 82, 129, 135
Evolution, theory of, 55-56,
59
Exodus, 16, 24, 34, 35, 80
Ezra, 25

Family purity, laws of, 88
Female/male principle.
See Male/female principle
First Born. *See B'chorah*
Frank, Adolphe, 65-66
Freud, Sigmund, 66

Gender, principle of, 61-62
Genesis, 16, 22, 25, 45, 129
see also Creation
Gregorian calendar, 27
Gurdieff, Georges, 67

Habiru, 16
Halevi, Z'ev ben Shimon, 62,
63, 65
Hebrew calendar, 25-26,
27-28
Hegel, Georg Wilhelm, 68
Heh, 26, 93
Hermes Trismegistus, 60-61
Hermetic Order, 60, 63
Hermetic Principles, 61-62, 68
Hermetic Society, 60
Hillel Rivlin of Schklov, 132

I Ching, 64
Inner Spiritual Soul, 30, 31, 32
Intellectual Soul, 30, 31
Isaac, 16, 65, 79
Israelites, 24-25

Jacob, 16, 25, 65, 79, 94
Jantsch, Erich, 58
Jeremiah, 91
Jesus of Nazareth, 48
Jew, definition of, 80-81, 88

Jewish Woman. *See* Woman
Joseph, 16, 65, 79
Jung, Carl Gustav, 66

Kabbalah, 37, 39, 65, 130
cosmic energy, 47
creation, interpretation of,
55
foundation for astrology, 66,
67
"Four Worlds," 57-58
Great Serpent, 33, 34
Lurianic *Kabbalah*, 137, 138
Perennial Philosophy and,
52-69
science and, 131-32, 139
Sefer Yetzirah, 26, 53, 54
"shells of concealment,"
32-33
Zohar, 56, 93, 128, 129, 131,
134, 137, 138
Kabbalah Connection, The
(Berg), 67
Kaplan, Aryeh, Rabbi, 26, 54,
63
Kashrut, 88, 89
Kiddush Hachodesh, 35, 36
Knowledge, unified theory of,
43-46, 53, 54
Kol Hator, 131-32, 134, 135-36,
137-38
Kybalion, 61

Leah, 79
Leonardo da Vinci, 48
Light, 45
Lunar calendar, 17, 25, 35, 37
Luxor-Karnak, 18

Maimonides, Moses, 30, 31-32,
81
Male/female principle, 22,
26-27, 28, 58, 82, 89
Mascaro, Juan, 62, 63
Mashiach. See Messiah
Meditations and Kabbalah
(Kaplan), 54

ABOUT THE AUTHOR

Susan Roth is a direct descendant of the Baal Shem Tov, through his great-grandson Rabbi Nachman of Breslov, the famous Kabbalist and scholar. She is also a direct descendant of the first Lubavitcher Rebbe, Shneur V. Zalman of Liadi, through his daughter Freida.

She has traveled extensively throughout the world since she was 7 years old, as a member of her family's Yiddish theatrical company, The Four Bursteins, and starred on stage, television, films and various radio programs and recordings throughout Europe, North America, Central America, South America, South Africa and Israel. She was also the youngest ventriloquist in the world and speaks six languages. She was introduced to Kabbalah at the age of 16 in Israel's Holy Mystical City of Safed.

She retired from the theater at the age of 19, and went on to raise a family. While doing so, she embarked on an unusual academic course of study. Beginning with a course in Liberal Arts at Union College in New Jersey, she continued her undergraduate studies in Philosophy and Comparative Religion at Kean College in New Jersey. She then received her Bachelor of Arts degree in the Humanities at Thomas Edison College of New Jersey ("The School Without Walls") and continued on with graduate studies in International Affairs as a Woodrow Wilson Scholar at Princeton University. She went on to receive her Master's degree in Liberal Arts from New York University, where she wrote her thesis in Perennial Philosophy through Kabbalah.

Before she began her academic studies, she worked in the following areas: as a coordinator of 2 political campaigns for New Jersey candidates; a freelance correspondent for community newspapers; vice president of the Women's Division of the Jewish Federation of Central New Jersey and the YM-YWHA; advisor, coordinator, speechwriter and public relations manager for the Central New Jersey Holocaust Committee, the Central New Jersey YM-YWHA, and the Central New Jersey Jewish Federation. She also broke ground as the first woman vice president of an Orthodox Synagogue.

She is a member of the World Future Society, the Noetic Society, and is active in the International Peace Center on Mt. Zion, Jerusalem, Israel.

Moses in the Twentieth Century is Susan Roth's first book. She currently resides in Westfield, New Jersey with her husband, Michael. They have two grown children.

ABOUT THE ANNOTATOR

Rabbi Moshe Ben-Yehudah is one of the most proficient scholars in Kabbalah today. He lives with his wife and children in Israel, where he teaches and lectures on the subject.